# Gerbils

# Complete Care Made Easy™

# Gerbils

## The Complete Guide to Gerbil Care

### By Donna Anastasi

photographs by Ellen Bellini

# BOWTIE PRESS®

Irvine, California

Karla Austin, *Business Operations Manager*
Nick Clemente, *Special Consultant*
Jarelle S. Stein, *Editor*
Jennifer Perumean, *Assistant Editor*
Jill Dupont, *Production*
Alleen Winters, *Book Designer*
Kenneth Brace, *Indexer*

Library of Congress Cataloging-in-Publication Data
Anastasi, Donna.
  Gerbils / by Donna Anastasi ; photographs By Ellen Bellini.
    p. cm. -- (Complete care made easy)
  Includes bibliographical references.
  ISBN 1-931993-56-4
  1. Gerbils as pets. I. Title. II. Series.

  SF459.G4A63 2005
  636.935'83--dc22
              2005001636

BowTie Press®
A Division of BowTie, Inc.
3 Burroughs
Irvine, California 92618

Printed and bound in Singapore
10 9 8 7 6 5 4 3 2 1

# Acknowledgments

MY THANKS TO MY DAUGHTERS AMY AND KATIE—WHO gave me the perfect excuse for getting our first two gerbils Blossom and Cara (the matriarchs of our ABC Gerbils clan)—and to my husband, Tom, for all of his supportiveness. For the completeness and quality of materials, I thank major reviewers Libby Hanna (Shawsheen River Gerbils), Tana Lyman (the Little Rascals), and Dr. Ann-Marie Lind; Tom Anastasi Jr., for detailed editing; and quick reviewers Gary Marfisi (Gary's Gerbils) and Cara-lee Lafond (the New York Gerbil [and more]). Thanks to Renee Arena (Cheesel's Burrow) for the section on adopting gerbils from the humane society and to Janet Morrow (Mountain Ash) for the color compilation picture graphics. For educating me about gerbils over the years and the many resources referenced within, I want to acknowledge Janet Morrow, president of the American Gerbil Society, and Julian Barker of the National Gerbil Society. For her amazing photography and dedication, I am deeply grateful to Ellen Bellini. And finally my thanks to BowTie Press, especially Assistant Editor Jennifer Perumean. —D.A.

My thanks to Libby, Stephen, Ruth, and Caroline Hanna; Ann-Marie, Ron, and Will Lind; Danielle, Damon, Damon Jr., and Devin Alexander; Kecia Santerre; Kelly and Savannah Greene; Matthew Hewitt; Dr. Nancy Kalb; Christine and Wayne Stys; Ms. Davies and her class; Megan and Maggie Connelly; Andy and Dimitra Milas; Tom Arena; Laurie Saisi; Nicky Gallant; Amy and Katie Anastasi; and Rebecca Fagan for allowing me to photograph them and their gerbils. My thanks to Donna Anastasi for her help and guidance. And special thanks to my husband, Jon, for his love, support and gerbil wrangling. —E.B.

# Contents

# 1

# Furry Mongolian Friends

This pair of nutmeg gerbils loves to explore a natural habitat.

COMPANION ANIMALS COME IN ALL SIZES AND OFFER many benefits: they bring us joy, reduce stress, build confidence, and teach responsibility. Pets have various needs as well, and it may not always be feasible to keep a pony, a dog, or even a cat. Gerbils, however, are pets almost anyone can keep. They are fun-loving, furry friends with endless energy and a talent for making people smile. They are also quiet, clean, friendly, curious, active, and easy to please. Gerbils have a natural liking for people and are especially fond of their own. If you are looking for a seemingly limitless cache of cuteness—from their long, fanning whiskers and large almond-shaped eyes to their bunnylike hind legs and tufted tail tips—then gerbils are for you!

# Just the Facts

Gerbils are mammals (*Mammalia*) under the order of rodents (*Rodentia*). They are in the same suborder as mice and rats (*Myomorpha*) and the same family as hamsters (*Cricetidae*). They are sometimes confused with mice, hamsters, or rats, but if you look closely, you'll notice several physical differences. A gerbil is bigger than a mouse, smaller than a rat, and about the size of an adolescent or small hamster. Unlike a hamster, the gerbil has a long tail; and unlike a rat or mouse tail, the gerbil's tail is fully furred with a thick tuft at the end. When not in motion, gerbils typically stand up on their haunches, rather than crouch down on all fours.

Pet gerbils come in more than 20 recognized color varieties, including the Dove, Lilac, Argente, and spotted Argente varieties shown here.

Gerbils have a life span of about three and a half years. They have a 4-1/2-inch-long body with a tail the same length. An adult female weighs as little as 2-1/2 ounces. An adult male, especially one that overindulges in sunflower seeds, can weigh as much as 4 ounces. Gerbils have a 1-1/2-inch midline scent gland, a vertical slit running up their bellies, which they use to recognize each other and also to scent-mark their territory. (The smell is imperceptible to us.)

Though gerbils have an appearance similar to that of other pet rodents, their wild origins, behavior, and history as pets are all their own.

# Wild Origins: Home on the Mongolian Range

The Mongolian gerbil is the gerbil species commonly kept as a pet in the United States. Mongolian gerbils are a type of jird (sometimes called sand rats, desert rats, yellow rats, antelope rats, or clawed jirds). Though less common, other related species kept as pets are the bushy-tailed jird, Egyptian gerbil, duprasi (fat-tailed gerbil), and Libyan jird.

Mongolian gerbils originated in northern China and, not surprisingly, Mongolia. Though dubbed "gentle gerbil" by the researchers who work with them, their Latin name is *Meriones unguiculatus*, or "clawed warrior", because, they are fiercely protective of home and family against gerbil strangers and other threats. (The teeth are the primary weapon in occasional battle; the claws are mainly for digging.) A typical family clan consists of an adult male and an adult female with up to three litters.

The Mongolian plain has temperature extremes: it can be a frigid 40 degrees below zero in the dead of a winter's night and can bake in a scorching high of up to 120 degrees in the noontime midsummer sun. Gerbils are perfectly suited to their harsh semi-desert grassland environment because they conserve heat with a compact body, furred tail with a tuft at the end, and small ears that are covered with thick, fine fur. In the wild, they retreat into their burrows to nap when it gets cold or hot, thus avoiding excessive temperatures.

Gerbils have many defense mechanisms. They have large internal middle and inner ear parts to hear low-frequency sounds such as those made by a predatory snake in the grass or an eagle owl hunting overhead. They also live in large groups where many watchful eyes check for danger; thumping feet signal clan members to dive for cover. In addition, gerbils can leap several inches off the ground or dodge sideways to avoid a creeping predator. But, when captured, if biting and clawing aren't enough, a gerbil can escape the clutches of an owl's talons by leaving behind only a piece of the tail, which is built to detach in the middle. As a final defense, wild gerbils have naturally occurring seizures, which enable them to twitch and then freeze (or play dead) under conditions of extreme stress.

Gerbils have muscular hind legs and large feet that are used not only for escaping from predators but also for digging burrows. They use their claws and strong, short front legs to loosen the dirt and then kick it out of the tunnel with their powerful hind legs. The wild gerbil's burrow is 12 feet or more across and is composed of nesting rooms lined with leaves, fur, and feathers for sleeping and birthing pups; storage rooms for holding food; and other chambers—all connected by tunnels. The burrow has several entrances, and the youngsters and most females usually do not venture too far from the escape routes.

Male gerbils claim the territory around the burrow (from one-quarter to one full square mile) by scent-marking the borders and chasing away intruders. In the summer, gerbils run great distances above ground every day, gathering and storing food. They sleep in small nest chambers located about 18 inches underground. In the winter, to keep warm, gerbils snooze in deeper nests, sometimes as much as 5 feet underground. They stay inside the burrow, eating seeds, grains, and other stored food for extended periods of time to escape the wind and cold.

The color of Mongolian gerbils in the wild is called Agouti (ah-GOO-tee), also called wild Agouti or golden Agouti, and is similar to a wild rabbit's coloration. The fur on the body is brown and gold, with black ticking or hair tips. The belly color is white or light gray. In addition to Agouti, pet gerbils come in a variety of colors. Unlike rats, rabbits, mice, and hamsters, domestic

A curious agouti gerbil uses large eyes, long full whiskers, and excellent hearing to explore.

This male gerbil scent marks by dragging his belly and scent gland on the ground leaving an oily residue to claim his territory as his own.

gerbils have no special coat types (there are, for example, no rex, long hair, or hairless gerbils), body mutations (there are no tail-less, lop, or dumbo-eared types), nor variation in size (there are no dwarf or giant sizes). Except for color, pet gerbils retain the appearance, as well as the good health and hardiness, of their ancestors found in the wild.

# History as Pets: The New Rodent on the Block

Of the "magnificent seven"—gerbils, hamsters, mice, rats, rabbits, ferrets, and guinea pigs—gerbils are the newest species to be introduced into the United States and to gain popularity as pets. In 1935, twenty breeding pairs of Mongolian gerbils were captured and imported into Japan where they were successfully bred in captivity. In 1954, this line of gerbils was exported to the United States for research: gerbils first arrived here, not as pets, but as laboratory animals.

In the lab, rumor has it that these normally agile tunnelers slacked off in the maze trials, preferring to focus their energy on endearing themselves to the young, soft-hearted research assis-

# Unique Gerbil Behaviors

**GERBILS MAY RESEMBLE OTHER POCKET PETS, BUT THEY** *don't always act like them. For example:*

- 1. **Gerbils are crepuscular:** Most rodents are nocturnal (awake all night). Gerbils are neither strictly nocturnal nor diurnal (awake only in the day). Instead, they are crepuscular. This means they are nappers who switch off between activity and sleep throughout the twenty-four-hour cycle. Their deepest sleep occurs at midday and midnight.

- 2. **Gerbils are social:** Unlike the solitary hamster, gerbils are social animals who depend on others of their own kind for their sense of safety and well-being, as well as for warmth and companionship. A same-sexed pair, either two males or two females, are the best of friends. A male and female breeding pair mate for life, and male gerbils are nurturing fathers who raise the babies with the mother.

- 3. **Gerbils are enthusiastic chewers:** Although all rodents need to chew to wear down their constantly growing teeth, when it comes to gnawing, gerbils are in a class all their own. Gerbils are avid gnawers that will demolish anything made of cardboard or wood. They can chew through hard plastic and have been known to take on ceramics, too!

tants. A typical account of gerbil temperament and behavior in the lab is written in a 1975 issue of *Gerbil Digest* by D. J. Robinson Jr.:

> Gerbils are certainly the most pleasant of all laboratory animals to handle, even for the novice. When their cage is opened, their curiosity impels them to come

to the opening where they may be picked up readily. They can be scooped up in one's palm and usually remain there without restraint.

## Gerbils in the Laboratory

*TODAY, LESS THAN 1 PERCENT OF ALL RODENTS USED IN research are gerbils. When scientists choose gerbils as laboratory subjects, they do so mainly for specialized purposes, such as studies on strokes, lipid metabolism, and epilepsy. Naturally occurring seizures are a hereditary trait that can be bred in or out of gerbils (and have been bred out of most pet gerbils). Researchers also use gerbils for auditory research, since gerbil hearing is similar to human hearing.*

Whether escaping the laboratory was a calculated move is up for debate, but two facts remain. First, American scientists became enamored with these fearless, friendly animals and began taking them home as pets for themselves and their children. Second, over time, gerbils developed a reputation for being "too curious" and exploratory for mazes and other behavioral studies. (Chapter 8 will reveal the secrets to motivating your gerbils to perform all sorts of tricks, including running a maze).

In 1964, gerbils traveled to the United Kingdom, where their popularity with hobbyists soared and resulted in breeding for color mutations, the establishment of gerbil color standards, and exhibiting gerbils in the first gerbil shows. Pet gerbils, the descendents of those original forty wild gerbils captured in Mongolia and imported to Japan more than seventy years ago, are now available worldwide.

This nutmeg gerbil stretches to climb up a branch. Providing your gerbils with a climbing branch or structure will let you see what agile creatures they are.

# 2

# Are Gerbils the Right Pets for You?

This toddler and her gerbils enjoy watching one another through the glass, but children under five may be too young to handle gerbils.

GERBILS MAKE GREAT PETS FOR JUST ABOUT ANYONE. They are charming little animals, like no other. They are easy to keep, entertaining to watch, and always ready for action. They are also surprisingly intelligent. Each has his own distinct personality, knows and loves his owner, and can be taught to climb up your arm and onto your shoulder. Observing your gerbils can impart life lessons, such as how to be a dedicated parent, how to be a devoted lifelong friend, and how to enjoy every moment to the fullest.

Clowns? Ha! Everybody loves gerbils! Young children enjoy watching their gerbils' antics as they play in their housing. An older child can actually enter the gerbils' world by sitting with them in a tub lined with a beach towel (no water, of course—gerbils don't stink, but they do sink). The teenage gerbil owner might want to create an elaborate gerbil housing complex. And, many adults are discovering for themselves the joys of gerbil companionship. Apartment dwellers, busy professionals, or those who frequently travel find that a pair of gerbils fit nicely into their lifestyles.

In addition, keeping gerbils provides an opportunity for meeting other gerbil enthusiasts. The American Gerbil Society in the United States and the National Gerbil Society in the United Kingdom are established organizations that provide active E-lists and hold online and live gerbil shows. They also distribute informative newsletters and offer many other resources.

Though gerbils are among the nicest and easiest pets to keep, it is still a good idea before taking on the responsibilities of gerbil ownership to determine what is involved. This chapter answers the most common questions and concerns about keeping gerbils, including:

- Do I have the right place, money, and time to keep pet gerbils right now?
- Are they good pets for children?
- Are they good classroom pets?
- Will they get along with my other pets?
- Who will care for them when I go on vacation?
- Are they subject to any special laws?

# A Place for Gerbils

Though housing for a gerbil pair takes up very little space, it is important that you give them the right place. Gerbils need to live indoors in a moderate temperature range (68 to 78 degrees).

Gerbils look lovely by a window; just keep them out of direct sunlight and drafts.

Since they come from a dry environment, living in a damp area like a basement is out. They'll need a place away from drafts and direct sunlight and one that's not too close to heaters or windows. Don't put the housing directly on the floor where the temperature can fluctuate widely. Your gerbils' home needs to rest on a sturdy piece of furniture or on a stand.

An ideal location for gerbils is one where they can watch you engaging in your daily activities and where you can frequently look in on them. Your gerbils will feel like part of your family, and you'll be able to quickly discover if there's a problem—for example, a water bottle that needs replenishing or a change in a gerbil's state of health.

Think twice about locating the gerbils in a young child's bedroom or playroom. Children may mishandle gerbils when not being supervised by a parent. A safer bet is a living or family room, an office, or even a landing or wide hallway.

A 10-gallon aquarium with a place to hide and plenty to do provides a perfect home for two gerbils.

Unless you're a heavy sleeper, plan to keep your gerbils in a room other than your bedroom, or be prepared to move them into the hallway at night. Those happy gerbil noises that entertain in the day may annoy the stuffing out of you at bedtime! Though gerbils are nonvocal, they gnaw, dig, drink from the water bottle, and run the wheel. In short, a couple of gerbils can be very loud in the still of the night.

If you do keep your gerbils in the bedroom, don't play with them, feed them, or give them cardboard before bedtime. Even rearranging the toys or turning a box upside down causes a great deal of excited scurrying and digging in the gerbil tank. Wheels can be hung on the side of the gerbil tank so they flip outside the enclosure at night; consider doing this to keep the noise level down.

# Cost

Gerbil supplies and accessories are easy to obtain. Online pet suppliers (even with shipping fees) and discount department stores offer great deals. Super pet stores provide immediate access to a wide variety of supplies, often at good prices. Smaller pet stores will typically have specialty items, as well as knowledgeable staff and top-quality animals. Since prices vary greatly, shop around if money is an issue.

The total cost of purchasing a pair of gerbils, basic housing, and necessities is about $75, broken down as follows:

- Two gerbils cost about $20.
- A basic gerbil housing setup starts at about $40.
- A wheel or other toy ranges from $5 to $10 (or more).
- Food, bedding, and incidentals are about $10 a month.
- Cardboard tubes and boxes are a gerbil staple and are free if recycled from home goods.

While it is unlikely that your gerbils will ever require medical attention, it is important to prepare for unexpected vet expenses. Gerbils still are considered "exotics" by many veterinarians, so the office visit alone could be $50 or more. As a rule of thumb, it is wise to have $100 on reserve should one of your gerbils fall ill, become injured, or (though unlikely) need to be euthanized.

## Time

It is important to check on your gerbils at least once a day. Gerbils need to be fed every day or every other day, and they require a regular supply of fresh water and a working water bottle. Checking on, caring for, and playing with your gerbils will take a minimum of fifteen minutes a day. The housing should be cleaned out every two weeks.

Talking to your gerbils when you pass by, resting your hand in the enclosure when you feed them, and taking your gerbils out at least a couple of times a week—even if you have just five minutes free—will keep them friendly and attached to you. Of course, gerbils would love more time out of their housing. In fact, the more time, the better. Gerbils especially enjoy the opportunity to dash full speed in an open space (one that is indoors and escape-proof). As long as they are gently and properly handled, with breaks to eat, drink, and nap, there is no such thing as too much attention.

## Gerbils and Other Pets

Never try mixing gerbils with another species. Gerbils cannot live with or play in the company of any other pets! Gerbils are territorial and will vigorously protect their home, turf, and clan

Gerbils have no natural fear of cats so it is important that the tank is clipped and cats are never left in a room alone with gerbils.

from other small animals, such as hamsters and guinea pigs. Ferrets will hunt your gerbils.

It is important to have a place in your house where gerbils can be kept out of reach from toddlers, ferrets, dogs, and cats. (Cats love gerbils but, unfortunately, they like them best as an entrée with a little catnip on the side.) Since gerbils have no natural fear of these potential predators, it is important that the gerbils are never allowed to run loose around them. However, as long as the gerbils are kept safely inside their housing, they will provide hours of "gerbil TV" to an enthralled audience. If you have especially persistent gerbil pursuers that are not content to

Time out of his housing is a highlight in this gerbil's day. Plan to spend at least 15 minutes a day feeding and playing with your gerbils.

simply look and not touch, you will have to clip or lock the tank cover or keep your gerbils in a room that is off-limits.

## Children and Gerbils

Gerbils can make excellent small companion animals for children. Without adult supervision, however, gerbils and young children are potentially harmful to each other. For example, a gerbil may be treated as an action figure rather than as a living being. However, unlike GI Joe, GI Gerbil will battle back under duress. And, repeated rough handling may cause your gerbil to develop a nipping habit. In general, gerbils may be too small and quick for children under five to handle, and children younger than ten are likely to need an adult nearby when the gerbils are out.

As with pets of any size, gerbils work best as a shared parent-child responsibility. Under a parent's watchful eye, youngsters will avoid committing common gerbil-handling faux pas: hugging and holding their gerbils too tightly; yelling and shrieking in their ears (gerbils have very sensitive hearing); dropping or stepping on them; and tugging on or even pulling off their detachable tails. Parents may be tempted to buy gerbils "for the kids," but the parent or other adult must be responsible for their care and for ensuring that children don't inadvertently hurt or kill their pets from neglect or from too much "loving."

## Gerbils in the Classroom

Gerbils, because they are outgoing and friendly, are good classroom pets if placed in the right circumstances: kept in a secure classroom by a gerbil-savvy teacher. Primary school teachers tell me that gerbils serve as icebreakers, ease school anxiety, and can

Having gerbils as their classroom pets offers these children both enjoyment and learning opportunities.

calm an upset child. Mrs. Deborah Davies, who teaches a class combined with first and second graders in Bedford, Massachusetts, says children are empowered by the responsibility of caring for animals who are totally dependent on them. Another practical benefit for teachers: gerbils, with their sensitive hearing, provide a compelling reason to keep the noise level down.

When considering gerbils as school pets, it is important to assess the safety of the classroom. Can the gerbils be kept securely in their housing and out of reach of young children? Is the room locked in the evening to prevent any unsupervised handling of the animals, or even abuse, from older children? Is the room temperature controlled (between 68 and 78 degrees) during the school's off-hours?

## A Better Bet for a Classroom Pet

**THOUGH A HAMSTER IS A MORE COMMON CLASSROOM** pet, gerbils have several advantages in the classroom:

- They're awake during school's normal day hours.
- They're busier and more athletic, exhibiting a wider range of behaviors.
- As social animals, two of them will play, groom, and cuddle together.
- They are easier to keep clean: their tank is less smelly and doesn't need to be cleaned out as often.
- They don't stress out as easily and are less likely to bite when under stress.

# Vacations

Gerbils do fine on their own for two to three days. Ample food and water should be provided, as well as a vegetable or fruit for liquid in case the water bottle runs dry. If you're going away for more than three or four days, hire a pet sitter to check on your gerbils or leave them with a friend. Unless the pet sitter has practiced holding the gerbils and you are confident they cannot escape, as a precaution ask that the gerbils stay inside their housing when others are caring for them.

Of course, you could always bring your gerbils on vacation with you! They are easy to take along and will be happy campers living in a smaller temporary space, as long as they have deep litter (about 3 inches), a nest box, and some cardboard. If you keep them in a plastic critter cage, check it often to make sure they're not chewing their way out. Frequent travelers may want

Consider bringing your gerbils with you on vacation. Gerbils are easy to take along and always ready for new adventures. (But don't bring them to the beach or let them loose outdoors no matter how much they beg!)

Gerbils travel well and make themselves right at home in temporary, smaller quarters, as long as they have deep litter, a place to hide, food and a carrot or other source of liquid. Make sure to purchase sturdy, gnaw-proof travel housing.

to purchase sturdier accommodations for their traveling gerbils—for example, a 2-1/2-gallon glass aquarium with a fitted mesh screen cover, or a wire cage with a deep pan on the bottom.

Most gerbils enjoy car rides and continue their normal gerbil activities while on the road. However, be sure to remove the water bottle during the drive (or it will bang and drip) and provide a carrot for liquid. When you stop to rest, give the gerbils a chance to drink from their water bottle, so they don't become dehydrated. Another way to give liquids when traveling is to spritz the side of the travel tank with a small spray water bottle; your gerbils will lick the water droplets right off the glass.

It is important to check with your transportation carrier—bus line, train, or airline—before attempting to board with your gerbils. Since the Transportation Security Act was passed, airport

## Did you know?

**NO MATTER WHAT THE CLIMATE, NEVER LET A GERBIL** *loose outdoors! Pet gerbils are not equipped to survive on their own; so if yours are released or get lost outside, they will die an unpleasant death from dehydration, starvation, or exposure, or be killed as prey within a few days. Help your gerbils live their full life span: keep them inside in a secure, protected enclosure.*

screeners will no longer look the other way when the occasional pocket pet shows up as a stowaway pocketbook pet on their screens. So, ask about the carrier's policy regarding gerbils when you make your plans. It would be heartbreaking to have to choose between deserting your beloved pets and forfeiting your vacation. Similarly, it may be easy to sneak gerbils into a hotel, but it is better to check with hotel management first. Often hotels that don't allow dogs and cats are happy to accommodate gerbils, though they may charge you a small fee.

## Gerbils and the Law

Having pet gerbils is illegal in the states of California and Hawaii, where they are seen as a threat to agriculture or the ecosystem (if released into the wild). If states with similar temperature ranges and terrain as California and Hawaii continue to find they have no problems with rampant feral gerbils, perhaps the laws for these two states will change. Unfortunately, for now, keeping gerbils is not an option for California or Hawaii residents. If you plan on vacationing in either one of these sunny spots, you'll need to leave your gerbils at home.

# 3

# Finding the Gerbils of Your Dreams

Young children, like this five-year-old, relate to their gerbils' antics and develop a strong affection for them.

CONGRATULATIONS! YOU'VE READ UP ON GERBILS AND have decided this is the perfect pet for you. Now comes the fun part: finding the gerbils of your dreams. It is critical to select gerbils that are healthy, tame, socialized, and confident. Therefore, it is important to know where to find nice ones, what questions to ask, what observations to make, and how to ensure that (unless you are planning to breed gerbils) you're really buying two males or two females.

## Where to Shop for Gerbils

When my daughters and I were ready to bring home our first gerbil pair, we automatically headed for the closest pet store; we didn't realize there were other places where we could have obtained our gerbils. You may be lucky enough to live around the corner from a good pet store with a knowledgeable staff, but there are many other places where you can find gerbils, such as a hobby breeder, humane society, or an individual. Keep in mind when searching for gerbils that gerbil babies—called pups—are indeed cute, but the baby stage lasts only a few weeks. A friendly pair that is already a few months old will likely make better pets than overly timid pups.

## Hobby Breeder

A small-scale hobby breeder usually has rarer-colored gerbils and more color variety—and has also spent time handling the pups, from birth. Some provide a pedigree that shows the lineage. And you can usually meet the gerbils' parents and grandparents. (Like most other species, gerbils tend to have personalities similar to those of either their mothers or fathers.) Breeders are usually happy to spend time dispensing information about the animals, gained from their own experiences with them. If gerbils are new to you, a breeder can show you how to handle and care for them. To find a local breeder, try an Internet search on "gerbils" and the name of your state. Or, search "gerbil breeders." The American Gerbil Society offers a state-by-state online listing of breeders.

## Shelters and Rescue Groups

While it is not as common with gerbils as with dogs and cats, there are owners who cannot keep their gerbils, so they bring them to a local shelter. If you're adopting gerbils from a shelter,

Often times a breeder will offer more color variety and rare-colored gerbils than those found at a pet store. No matter where you get them, handle the gerbils to make sure they have been tamed and are friendly before bringing them home.

Humane societies sometimes offer small animals such as gerbils in addition to dogs and cats. You do not need to get young gerbils to have them bond with you; adult gerbils that have been tamed at a young age make excellent pets.

you will have to fill out a form with pertinent information, including whether you own or rent your home. If you rent, you may be asked to provide proof that pets are allowed by your landlord. If it is the first time you've adopted from the shelter, they may ask to see your housing setup for your gerbils or to meet all other pet caregivers in the home, including children. These things are done as precautions. The shelter staff loves animals and wants to find good homes for them; they do not want these adopted animals returned to them, especially since they'll be older and perhaps have newly acquired behavioral issues. They may want to know how knowledgeable you are about gerbil care. A staff member will likely teach you the basics or give you some printed information to take home. The fee for adopting gerbils from shelters can vary widely, but usually it is between $5 and $20 per animal.

Animal shelters that have limited small animal facilities will need interested individuals to call if gerbils are surrendered to them. You might leave your number to be contacted when such an opportunity arises. They may have a bulletin board where people can leave advertisements for gerbils, and you may be able to post one for "Gerbils Wanted."

A rescue group is a collection of individuals who take in a specific type of animal with the intention of finding them permanent homes. Some shelters are not equipped to take in small animals, or the staff may not be experienced with them; so they rely upon rescue groups to give these animals a foster home until a permanent family can be found. Typically, shelters and rescue groups work closely together, so even though the local shelter may not have gerbils, they may know of a local rescue group that does. Since shelters and rescue groups often work with veterinarians, one in your area may also be a good resource to help you find gerbils looking for a home. The Rat and Mouse Club (RMCA.org) has an online list of veterinarians who have experience in treating rodents.

## Pet Stores

Most pet stores sell young gerbils, and some take in and adopt out donated adult gerbils, with their supplies, too. If you decide to buy your gerbils from the local pet store, call first! The pet store may be one that does not carry gerbils or may currently be out. When you call to ask if they have gerbils, also ask how many they have, how old they are, whether they are females or males, if they are friendly, and what colors they are. They may not know the official color names, but by asking about the gerbil's eye, belly, and back colors, you can figure out the color by using the color chart in this chapter. The male and female gerbils should be separated into their own tanks. Avoid buying gerbils, especially females, from a mixed gender tank; if a mature male is present, females more than eight weeks old are likely to be pregnant.

If nearby pet stores do not have gerbils and you cannot find a gerbil breeder, you can expand your pet store search online using Switchboard.com and entering "pet store" as the business and a "100-mile" distance from your start point.

## Other Places to Find Gerbils

There are gerbils out there looking for homes; the trick is to find them. Sometimes, home situations or life circumstances force the placement of a pet, so keep your eyes on the classified ads, especially in local newspapers and other publications. Super pet or pet supply stores, vet offices, feed and grain stores, and even supermarkets and Laundromats have bulletin boards where an ad for available gerbils might be posted.

There are online classified ads for gerbils, too, as well as sites dedicated to placing animals. Many types of small animals can be found online at Petfinder.org. Other resources include the American Gerbil Society and National Gerbil Society, both of which have online classified ads for gerbils in the United States who need homes.

# Pick of the Litter

When adopting a puppy, owners typically contact or visit a variety of kennels and spend time with the animals before selecting the pet they want. Consider investing a similar effort into finding the perfect gerbils. Driving several hours to a gerbil kennel in another state may seem like a lot of work (or even nutty to the uninitiated, so be prepared for an odd reaction from your co-workers if you tell them how you spent the weekend!). But, anyone who has experienced the deaths of baby gerbils after

This family looks for a pair of gerbils to make their own. Most breeders will have many gerbils in to pick from. When selecting gerbils as pets, find the friendliest gerbils and from these choose the colors you like. Both male and female gerbils make equally nice pets.

owning them for a few days, or who has owned gerbils who act too wild to hold, is likely to agree that dedicating a day to gerbil adoption is worth the effort.

No matter where you acquire your gerbils, it is important that the animals are healthy. Make sure the gerbils are comfortable being handled; if you are new to gerbils, have the seller hold them for you to see how they respond to people. Find gerbils that are tame and friendly. Ideally, they have been frequently and carefully handled so they like and trust people.

Gerbils between six and nine weeks are at a fun age; they're easy to tame and cute, too! If the seller doesn't know the age of the gerbils, you can use their size, weight, and tail length to estimate age. An adult gerbil is typically 4-$\frac{1}{2}$ inches, with a solid muscular body, and a tail the same length. A seven-week-old pup is about 25 percent smaller and much lighter than an adult, and their tails are a little bit longer than their bodies.

Be prepared to walk away if you have concerns about the gerbil's health or temperament. Look for slow-moving red or black dots on the side of the gerbil tank or on the fur of the animal near the skin; these are mites, and you should not bring home gerbils that have them or other parasites. If the gerbils are living in unsanitary conditions, continue your search elsewhere. This will avoid heartache on your part and will discourage irresponsible animal husbandry on the part of the person who is maintaining gerbils in such deplorable conditions.

## Colors, Varieties, and Availability

Health and temperament are the most important considerations when choosing gerbils. But, once you find a pet store or breeder with friendly, healthy gerbils, the next decision is color. Gerbils come in many colors. Some have a white belly; some are spotted. There are also colorpoint gerbils, such as Siamese, which means that the nose, paws, ears, and tail are a darker shade than the head and body, like a Siamese cat. Eyes are either black or a deep ruby color.

All gerbils between six and ten weeks "molt" into a new coat of fur. The new coat, for most colors, is the same or similar to their baby fur. However, some varieties undergo dramatic molts. For example, a nutmeg gerbil starts out as a rusty orange color and molts into black-ticked fur tips, giving the adult coat a brindled appearance, somewhat similar to an Agouti; a silver nutmeg starts out a cream color and molts into black-ticked fur tips making the coat look silver; Himalayan, Siamese, and Burmese gerbils are born without colorpoints, and the dark nose, ears, tail, and paws appear when they molt.

Six to nine weeks is a perfect age to adopt a pair of baby gerbils; insist on getting two that are healthy, curious, and sweet.

## Females or Males?

Both female and male gerbils make wonderful pets, as there are few gender-based differences in temperament or behavior. Male gerbils are about 25 percent larger than females, although they do not come into their adult male build until they reach six to ten months. Females tend to be more active and athletic and are quicker to scramble up your arm or leap to the rim of the tank at the slightest opportunity, while males are more likely to sit with you (although most gerbils, whether male or female, are too busy to be very cuddly!). If you need to introduce a lone gerbil, a male usually is easier to introduce, especially to a baby. All in all, though, individual personality will determine your gerbils' traits more than their gender. So, find gerbils you like, and peek underneath afterwards to see if you've got females or males. Just make sure you get two of the same!

# Questions to Ask the Seller

**HERE ARE A FEW PERTINENT QUESTIONS TO ASK, ALONG**
with corresponding observations to make:

● Are the gerbils healthy? (Is the fur shiny, sleek, and not puffed? Are the eyes bright, shiny, and open wide? Do the gerbils look like the pictures in this book?)

● Are the gerbils alert and active?

● Are they tame and friendly? (Rest your hand in the tank. Do they come to investigate? Will they climb into your hand? When touched, do they seem at ease, or do they flinch or run away? Certainly, they should not nip. Young babies may taste and mouth everything; this is not considered a nip. In fact, it tickles!)

● How old are the gerbils?

● Are they males or females? (Unless you want a litter of baby gerbils, make sure to get two of the same gender. Any male and female gerbils will mate—even brother and sister, parent and child.)

Sellers do not always know how to determine a gerbil's gender, so being incorrectly identified is common. In fact, the most frequent problem I receive through E-mail is, "Help! My gerbils just had babies." Sometimes, one or both females come home pregnant, but often the problem is that the pair consists of a male and female, instead of two of the same sex.

The one sure way to make sure the gerbil genders are as stated (and a "Bernard" does not turn out to be a "Bernadette") is to "sex" them yourself. First hold the gerbil upright so the belly is facing you. If the gerbil struggles too much, try putting him or

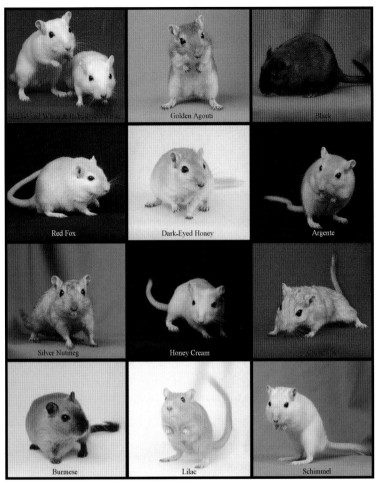

Here are some of the more than 20 gerbil colors available. Any colors can have spotted markings.

her in a small plastic or glass carrier and looking through the bottom at the gerbil's underside. Examine the distance between the urinary and anal openings. Whether male or female, every gerbil has two buttons. The button above pops out and is the genitalia, which looks the same for both sexes; the button beneath pushes in and is the anus or bum (a nervous baby may verify this by pooping while you're checking his or her gender). On a female, the two buttons are close together; for female pups, they are practically touching. On a male, there will be some distance between the buttons, as much as a half-inch, especially as he gets older. A male gerbil also has a small bulge to either side of the buttons (his scrotum). The bulges do not appear until the gerbil is about five weeks old. From six to seven weeks, the scrotum is furless and prominent, making it the easiest way to differentiate male and female gerbils at that age. At eight weeks, the scrotum gets covered with dark fur and isn't as noticeable.

## One Gerbil, Two Gerbils, Three Gerbils, More?

Gerbils are social animals and need a gerbil friend for security, grooming, and companionship. Lone gerbils can become irritable, skittish, lethargic, and obese. Gerbils kept in twos get along nicely, and this is the recommended arrangement, especially for first-time owners.

If keeping a larger colony of gerbils, make the housing setup simple, with only one hiding and sleeping spot. This way the gerbils are more likely to sleep together and are less likely to set up territories. Toys or a more elaborate setup for supervised play sessions are fine, as long as everything is cleaned in hot water between uses.

If you decide to keep three or more gerbils together, keep a close eye on them because they may fight once they hit maturity. If blood is drawn, you will have to split them into smaller groups. If you have a trio that fights, remove one of them and introduce her to another gerbil. The natural tendency is to take out the "bully," but I would recommend leaving the more dominant and aggressive gerbil with the one who was not involved in the

| Name of Color | Body Color | Belly Color | Eye Color | Availability |
|---|---|---|---|---|
| Agouti | Brown with black fur tips | White | Black | High |
| Argente | Orange | White | Ruby | High |
| Black | Black | Black | Black | High |
| Lilac | Deep gray | Gray | Ruby | High |
| Dove | Light gray | Light gray | Ruby | High |
| Nutmeg | Brown, orange and black mix | Cream, black fur tips | Black | High |
| Ruby-eyed white | White | White | Red or pink | High |
| Dark-eyed honey | Gold | White | Black | Moderate |
| Honey cream | White with orange dappling | White | Black | Moderate |
| Red fox | Reddish orange | Gold | Ruby | Moderate |
| Yellow fox | Yellowish gold | White | Ruby | Moderate |
| Himalayan | White, dark tail | White | Ruby | Moderate |
| Slate | Dark slate gray | Dark slate | Black | Rare |
| Chinchilla (gray Agouti) | Silver | White | Black | Rare |
| Silver nutmeg | Silver | Light gray | Black | Rare |
| Cinnamon (color point nutmeg) | Cinnamon (rust), white undercoat | Cream | Black | Rare |
| Black-eyed white | White | White | Black | Rare |
| Polar fox | White with beige fur tips | White | Black | Rare |
| Apricot polar fox | Apricot | White | Ruby | Rare |
| Siamese | Tan with brown nose, tail, paws | Tan | Black | Rare |
| Burmese | Chocolate, dark nose, tail, paws | Chocolate | Black | Rare |
| Schimmel | White with orange nose, tail | White | Black | Rare |

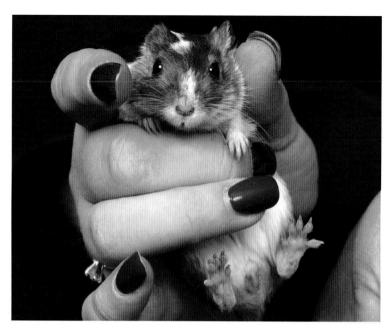

Above, a female gerbil's urinary "button" is almost touching or close to the anal opening. Below, a male gerbil will have a much farther separation, up to a half inch. Look for the scrotum's bulge on a male gerbil. You might be able to see this "extra package" from the side of a standing gerbil as well.

fight—because a more dominant gerbil can be harder to pair with another gerbil than a submissive one. If you didn't see the fight, look for the gerbil with more cuts on the tail and rump (this is the submissive gerbil), whereas the more dominant gerbil may have only a few cuts, with these on the face and neck area. To avoid all of these complications, simply keep two gerbils; they should live together peaceably their whole lives.

# Introducing Two Gerbils

Ideally, your two gerbils come from the same litter and will live out their lives together. However, if you purchase them from different sources or if one dies and you want to add a new one, they must be carefully and gradually introduced to each other.

The most important factor to successfully introducing two gerbils is their personalities: some gerbils are more accepting of unfamiliar gerbils than others. That said, age and gender factors tend to make certain introductions easier than others (see chart).

| Gerbils Being Introduced | Level of Difficulty |
|---|---|
| Six-week-old baby gerbils | Piece of cake |
| Adult male and a baby (or two) | Easy |
| Two young adult males | Moderate |
| Young female and a young male | Moderate |
| Two young females roughly the same size | Challenging |
| Older female and adult male | Challenging |
| Two older females | Super challenging |
| Adult female and a baby | Don't try it |
| Lone gerbil and established group | Don't try it |

A 7-week-old gerbil pup is about 75 percent the length of an adult, much lighter in weight, and has an immature appearance compared with the muscular, filled-out adult.

## Split Cage

When introducing two gerbils, precautions are necessary to avoid fighting, unless they are babies. Using a "split cage" allows the gerbils to learn each other's smell without exposing them to harm. You can build a split cage by dividing the tank with ¼-inch mesh wire cloth. Fasten it with masking tape (replace the tape as needed, since the gerbils will gnaw at it). If you are handy, you can secure metal channeling to the tank by using silicone aquarium sealant; this will hold the divider. There must be no way for even the most determined gerbil to get over, under, or around the divider! Put a brick or other heavy object on top of the tank lid so that the gerbils cannot push the lid up and climb over the divider.

Another way to create an introduction tank is to place a smaller cage inside a larger tank. For example, place a small wire cage inside the larger tank, or set a small 2-½-gallon tank with a mesh wire cover on its side.

When using a split cage, start with a clean tank and fresh litter. Then, put the gerbils in the split cage, one gerbil on each side of the divider. Provide no toys or accessories while introduc-

This split cage setup shows how to introduce two gerbils. Gerbils that are strangers or bonded gerbils that have been separated for more than 24 hours need to be introduced gradually and carefully in a divided cage where the two can smell, but not hurt, each other.

ing the gerbils; you don't want them to get territorial. Insert only unscented toilet tissue and a small cardboard box taped near the divider (so they nest, sleep, and gnaw close to one another). Swap the gerbils between sides (or enclosures) at least few times a day, the more often the better.

## Putting Them Together

When putting the two gerbils together, pick a day when you will be home to supervise. Place a thick glove nearby in case you need to slip it on quickly to break up a gerbil fight. Have a smaller cage on hand in case you need to separate the gerbils for a short time. Plan on carrying the tank from room to room with you. Do not take your eyes off the gerbils until they are successfully introduced.

After your two gerbils have been in the split cage for a week, take any boxes or other items out (so there are no territories or hiding places), swap the gerbils between sides one more time, and, after a few minutes, try removing the divider.

## When Introductions Go Wrong

Sometimes, two gerbils get off to a rocky start. For example, immediately after they are introduced, one gerbil may chase the other around the tank with the pursued gerbil leaping into the air to escape. Or, one may puff her fur and show her side to the other (in an attempt to look bigger and tougher) and push up against the other. They may engage in a "ball fight," which is like a fight you might see in a cartoon: two characters roll around in a ball with dust flying all over. Try to separate them before actual fighting begins.

Fighting gerbils are not ready to be introduced and need to spend another week in the split cage. When you reintroduce them, use a neutral tank—one that has been washed out and has clean litter—so it doesn't smell like either of the gerbils.

Maybe you are attempting a difficult introduction, such as finding an elderly female a new friend. Or you have two gerbils who, given age and gender, *should* get along but have incompatible temperaments and just don't seem to like each other. Before giving up, try your bonding-resistant gerbils at least two to three weeks more in the split cage. If you are convinced that this matchup is not going to work, you could try one or both with a different partner.

If you have a gerbil that cannot be introduced to another gerbil, she may be comforted by living near (if not with) other gerbils. The scurrying, digging, and thumping of gerbil neighbors lets her know she's not alone in the world. If this is the case, give this lone gerbil extra attention, a hiding "den," lots of cardboard, a wheel, and the opportunity to get out and run.

Gerbils that are fighting will circle each other and go for the side of the neck. Never put two unfamiliar gerbils together or they will fight. Separate fighting gerbils immediately before one or both are seriously injured.

## When Introductions Go Right

In a successful introduction, the gerbils first will lick mouths and sniff bottoms to identify each other. If they seem to be getting along without fighting, create a gerbil bonding experience: give them a scrap of cardboard to gnaw on (nothing they can hide in), provide a handful of food and treats in the center of the tank, or give them a pile of unscented toilet tissue to burrow (and, hopefully nest) in together. An unraveled toilet tissue tube offers a coil for gerbils to crawl through and a means of spreading their individual smells onto one another. (Make sure the tube doesn't provide a hiding spot.)

If your gerbils are familiar with each other but not fully introduced, you may want to place their tank in the middle of a busy house. With dogs barking, children yelling, and people

A dark-eyed honey and a honey cream youngster snuggle together. A gerbil that must sleep alone or out in the open feels vulnerable; this is stressful for a gerbil.

passing by, the two gerbils will become distracted from each other, and their natural tendency to stick together against the tough outside world will help them bond.

Sometimes, gerbils get along in the initial minutes of the introduction but will squabble or act uncomfortably with each other soon after. Pay close attention. If they're nervous, their motions may appear jerky rather than fluid. They may box with their front paws, groom too aggressively, squeak, or show other signs of uneasiness. In this case, determine which one is the more

## Did you know?

**NEVER PUT YOUR BARE HAND INTO A GERBIL FIGHT!**
While fighting, a gerbil's automatic reaction is to chomp on anything that touches her, and you will get bitten. If you are not wearing a glove, use anything you can grab (e.g., the water bottle, a shoe) and shove it between the two gerbils to separate them. If necessary, dump the entire contents of the tank—gerbils and all—onto the floor. Worry about the mess after the two gerbils are separated.

dominant or aggressive gerbil. The more submissive one is likely to remain in one corner while the more dominant one roams the tank. Put the more dominant gerbil in a "time-out." (Place her in a smaller escape-proof cage, located inside the tank near the corner where the other gerbil is settled.) A time-out can be fifteen to thirty minutes. Do this as many times as needed.

It's a good sign if your gerbils take only a mild interest in or ignore each other, seem relaxed, and are engaged in normal gerbil activities; or, when one gerbil, especially the larger one, lies flat (making her look smaller), closes her eyes, and lets the other groom her. Gerbils may at first settle in diagonally opposite corners of the tank, then move to separate corners on the short side of the tank, and finally move into the same corner and sit side by side. Once the gerbils are grooming one another and sleeping in the same nest, continue to check on them from time to time; but it is pretty certain they are friends. Congratulate yourself on completing a successful gerbil introduction!

# 4

# Housing and Feeding

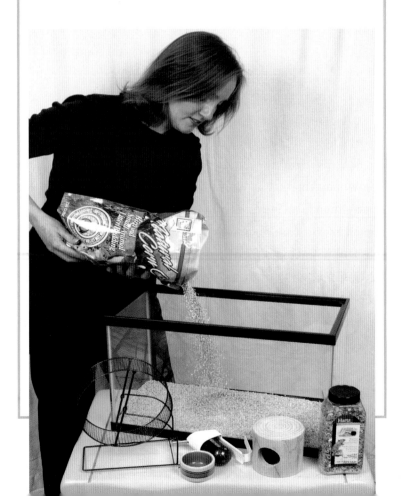

This little princess gerbil is playing in an aquarium decoration castle. If a basic setup just won't do, search not only the small animal section of the pet store but also the reptile, bird, and fish sections for gerbil extras.

OF ALL THE SMALL COMPANION ANIMALS, THE GERBIL IS as low-maintenance a pet as you get. Gerbils take up little space—their home can fit neatly on a shelf, bureau, or desktop. They don't demand extensive time outside the cage for exercise and play. They love to come out, but they are also content to play inside their housing. Most other small animal cages require weekly cleaning with frequent partial or spot cleanings in-between; but since gerbils use water efficiently and produce very little waste, their housing can go two weeks between cleanings. Gerbils are easy to feed, too. You simply need to provide a handful of quality gerbil food every day or two and a water bottle filled with clean drinking water.

# Home Sweet Home

Before bringing your gerbils home, it is a good idea to prepare their housing for their arrival. (Having a new tank to explore will help the gerbils adjust more quickly.) If you have far to travel, you might want your gerbils to ride home in their permanent housing (if it is a manageable size); a sturdy box or travel cage will also work. Those flimsy cardboard carriers from the pet store won't hold your gerbils for long; they have a chew-through life of a half-hour or less if there are a couple of determined gerbils inside.

As a rule of thumb, provide 5 gallons of space per gerbil. A 10-gallon tank is an adequate size for a gerbil pair; if you decide to go bigger, your gerbils will enjoy the extra space. There are many types of housing available for gerbils: wire cages, plastic "habitrails," large plastic cages with snap-on plastic lids, and, arguably the best choice, glass aquariums.

Wire cages are adequate but block the viewing, and gerbils will kick litter out of the cage. Make sure the bars are close together, especially if gerbils are younger than nine weeks. Plastic cages eventually get dull and scuffed with gerbil scratches. Since gerbils are champion chewers, over time they may figure out a way to gnaw out of the plastic and escape. Housing your gerbils in an aquarium with a metal mesh tank cover has several advantages. You can keep the litter deep and your gerbils can dig and burrow in it without litter flying through wires slats and making a mess. Glass provides the best viewing of your gerbils' cuteness, and since they are fascinating to watch in their own environment, you'll appreciate this option. Tanks and covers are located in the fish or reptile section of a pet store.

Whatever type of housing you use, it is important to keep the gerbils out of drafts and direct sunlight. Gerbils in wire cages are especially susceptible to chills. Likewise, the glass in an aquarium may concentrate the heat from the sun, and this could kill your gerbils.

## Nice and Cozy: Basic Housing Setup

Be creative in your housing. The more you tap into the nature of your gerbils, the more varied behaviors you'll see and the happier they'll be. Gerbils like to dig, tunnel, nest, gnaw, climb, leap, and run. To provide for all your gerbils' basic needs— and avoid giving them harmful items—follow the handy shopping list on following page.

Basic gerbil necessities include a secure and roomy home with a place to sleep, exercise equipment, absorbent litter, a water bottle, and a quality commercial gerbil food mix.

# SHOPPING LIST

| What to Buy | Purpose | What to Avoid |
|---|---|---|
| 10-gallon tank | For adequate amount of space | Plastic housing; may not be escape-proof |
| Wire mesh cover with cover clips | For safety, especially if cats or toddlers are persistent | Plastic covers; may not be escape-proof |
| 4-ounce rounded-top water bottle with metal guard holder | To provide constant access to water and prevent being gnawed | Water bottles that hang too low; may touch the litter and drip |
| Food (16 percent protein for growing gerbils) | A varied seed mix provides nutrition and stimulation | Vitamins; provided by their food |
| Ceramic hideaway or wooden nest box | For hiding; place in the corner of the tank before adding litter | Plastic toys or nesting fluff; harmful if ingested |
| 8-inch solid or wire mesh wheel—or climbing structure with ramps or ledges | For exercise | Open slat wheel; can injure toes and tails |
| **Litter** | | |
| Processed paper (e.g., CareFRESH) Aspen Corncob | For digging and sanitation; provide 3 inches of deep, safe litter | Pine or cedar litter; can cause allergies and other more severe health problems |
| **What to Find at Home** | | |
| Hollow, tube-shaped toy or paper towel roll | For tunneling | Make sure the diameter of any tubes or holes are at least twice the size of your gerbils' heads so they won't get stuck |
| Unscented toilet tissue | For nesting | Cloth or fiber items: string can be harmful to toes or tummy if eaten |
| Cardboard | For gnawing; toss in a daily supply for your gerbils to demolish | Egg cartons and boxes from the refrigerator; may contain spoiled food |

## Living Large: Mansions and Palaces

If modest housing simply won't do for your gerbil royalty, consider creating a gerbil mansion or palace; they will love the extra real estate. A 20-gallon tank is a nice size and yet is still manageable for lifting. You can add a second story on top of a 10-gallon tank by buying a wire cage built specifically to fit. Since gerbils have a healthy fear of heights, make sure to keep the litter several inches deep so they see they don't have far to fall—and they'll discover that they don't get hurt if they do.

Though wire cages and plastic tubing housing may not be ideal as the primary residence, they make nice add-ons to an aquarium setup. A small wire cage placed on the floor of the tank makes a jungle gym for climbing and exploring. Plastic tubes inside a large aquarium are also a big hit. (These should be removed, and washed, after a few hours of playtime so that the gerbils won't get tired of tunneling and then switch to nibbling on them.) Some gerbil owners replicate a burrowing system by connecting tanks together with tubes. If you create an elaborate housing system, make sure you can maintain it. Gerbils will be happier in a tidy 10-gallon setup than in one three times larger and filthy because it's a chore to clean.

Gerbils have a blast on wooden structures and playgrounds. It may take some hunting around in specialty pet stores or on the Web to find an appropriate gerbil playground. If you enjoy carpentry, you can design and build one yourself, using wooden dowels, nontoxic Elmer's glue, or small dull-ended screws to connect the pieces. If you aren't handy, try giving your design to someone who is. The structure should have two or three levels, a few entry and exit points, and balconies and ledges. It should not be too elaborate or large (no more than one-third of your tank space). Ramps should

A tank topper is a quick way to double the real estate of a 10-gallon tank. Gerbils kept in stimulating housing are active and exhibit a wide variety of behaviors.

be gently angled with good traction so the gerbils don't fall or slip.

Gerbils especially enjoy a climbing "tree" (driftwood or branch). In the wild they build their burrows around the roots of a plant. Perhaps that's why gerbils love having a branch in the tank to climb on, nibble at, hide behind, and build nests and tunnels around. Unfortunately, you cannot just walk outdoors and pick up a nice stick. You may be introducing bugs, mold, or other unhealthy things into the tank, or it might be the wrong kind of wood. Kiln-dried fruit branches or driftwood pieces are beautiful to look at and safe for gerbils. These are available at pet stores and pet specialty shops or online. A nice piece can be expensive, but it will last a while. And, your gerbils will love you for it.

## Toys and Extras

Gerbils like toys, but they get confused if there are too many in the tank. While more toys all at once are overwhelming, regularly changing your supply of one or two toys will provide stimulation and variety. Just make sure to wash toys well between uses.

Gerbils like any toys they can climb on, in, over, and through. Ceramic toys will last longer than wood, but wooden toys are great, too, for playing on and gnawing! Some gerbil owners stay away from plastic toys altogether for fear that small pieces will be ingested (besides, plastic toys don't last very long). Others use them with supervision or for limited play sessions. Keep away from toys containing cloth or fiber, because the strings can wrap around and amputate toes and possibly cause intestinal problems if eaten.

Here are a few inexpensive gerbil extras to add to your shopping list:

- Chinchilla dust for baths (see Chapter 6)—after fluffing in a shallow bowl of chinchilla dust, your gerbil will be extra clean and soft.

- Alfalfa or timothy hay—gerbils will hide in it and nibble on it, and some hays make gerbils frisky and playful.

- Ceramic bowl—gerbils look adorable eating out of a little ceramic bowl.

- Roll-a-nest—these don't last long, but gerbils love popping out of the holes and dismantling these.

- Ceramic or wood log—a nice place to play, hide, and sleep.

- Run-around ball—if free runs are out of the question, this provides a safe way to let gerbils run.

A hollowed coconut makes a fun toy—and a nice bed. (A nest "box" doesn't have to be square.)

## Cardboard, Cardboard, Cardboard

If gerbils had a slogan, it would be "It's All About the Cardboard." No matter how much you spend on a fancy gerbil toy, your gerbils are guaranteed to get more excitement from the box the toy came in!

Here are some examples of toys your gerbil will love. The possibilities are endless when it comes to spoiling your gerbils with toys.

If possible, offer your gerbil cardboard every day. (He'll spend the next fifteen minutes to two hours enjoying it and destroying it.) At a minimum, give cardboard a few times a week; chewing cardboard or wood helps to wear down your gerbil's constantly growing front teeth. A few classic gerbil favorites are small, lightweight boxes (such as cereal boxes cut in half); toilet and paper-towel rolls; and those processed cardboard drink carriers (unused) from a fast food restaurant.

Don't use cardboard that has been in the refrigerator or freezer (which may contain food particles that could rot), especially egg cartons, which might cause salmonella. Don't offer cardboard that is wax-coated or that has strings embedded in it (found in some shipping boxes).

## Get in the Gerbil Zone

**ONCE YOU START THINKING LIKE A GERBIL, YOU'LL** realize that the gerbil-hamster section of a pet store is just one of many places where you can find the niceties of life for your gerbils. Don't confine yourself to the pet store's small-animal department; housing pieces for reptiles and toys for birds are also perfect for gerbils!

Heck, why even stop at the pet store? Once you are in the gerbil zone and have a sense of what gerbils like, you will find appropriate items everywhere you look: office supply stores (use wire mesh bookends for ledges by attaching them to the glass with aquarium repair silicone); hardware stores (possibilities with PVC pipes are endless); toy stores (specifically, preschool toys); yard sales; garden stores (at the end of the season, you can pick up inexpensive strawberry pots and other ceramics); and unfinished-wood stores (this is a gerbil toy paradise!).

This black, mottled gerbil is settling down for a good gnaw. Gerbils are avid chewers and like all rodents need a constant supply of cardboard and wood to wear down their continually growing front teeth.

# Speed Cleaning

Gerbils are one of many small animals that practice coprophagy. Politely, this means their excrement contains necessary nutrients and by ingesting their own pellets, a vitamin B deficiency is avoided. So, you don't want to clean out their tank too often. Gerbils also put much time and effort into creating tunnel structures and making their homes just so; therefore, overly frequent cleanings may be an unwelcome stressor. On the flipside, living on unsanitary bedding can make gerbils ill, so don't wait too long.

Clean out the entire gerbil tank every two weeks, or more frequently as needed. Use your nose as a guide; your gerbils' housing should not have a strong or unpleasant smell. If

The gerbils' housing should be cleaned out every two weeks. First, dump out the old litter. Clean the housing with very hot water and a drop of bleach or small animal cage cleaner. Rinse well. Make sure to dry the housing well; gerbils are desert animals that are sensitive to moisture and humidity.

bedding gets wet between cleanings, for example, from a leaky water bottle, remove the wet bedding and replace it with dry litter.

In addition to providing for all your gerbils' needs, a basic housing setup is quick and convenient to clean. Here's how to clean out a 10-gallon gerbil tank in fifteen minutes and in three easy steps. Before getting started, you will need a container to hold your gerbils (such as a clean, small plastic carrier), a large-size trash bag, a bathtub, a sink, a drop of bleach or detergent made for small animal cages, paper towels, fresh bedding, several new boxes or tubes, and masking tape.

**Step 1** (Approximate time: two minutes)

- Put your gerbils into a clean carrier with a little bedding and a bit of cardboard.

- Remove the water bottle and guard, toys, bowls, and exercise wheel from the tank or cage.

- Dump the soiled contents into the large trash bag.

**Step 2** (Approximate time, with some practice: ten minutes)

- Put all the toys back into the tank or cage and place it into the bathtub.

- With the stopper in place, put one small drop of bleach or other gerbil-safe detergent into the tank, and run a few inches of very hot water over the tank and toys.

- Rather than filling the tank to the top, dump the water into the tub and wash all four sides of the tank by flipping it over onto each side in the shallow water of the tub. Wash the tank top as well.

- Empty the tub and rinse the tank, again containing all items, with hot water.

- At the same time, wash the water bottle and food dish in very hot water in the sink (no bleach).

- Dry the inside of the tank, toys, and food dish with paper towels.

**Step 3** (Approximate time: three minutes)

- Put a new cardboard box or tube into the tank, return the toys and nest box, and cover everything with 3 inches of bedding.

- Fill the food dish.

- Fill the water bottle with fresh water.

- Hang the water bottle and wheel (with masking tape) on the side of the tank; if the wheel is open-slatted, cover the slats inside and out with masking tape, to avoid injuries to your gerbil's tail or feet.

- Return the gerbils to the tank and watch them race through and explore their new world.

## Keep It Clean

**ALWAYS WASH IN SCALDING HOT WATER ANY TOY OR** other equipment that is removed from the tank and later reintroduced; the stale gerbil smell might be confused with the smell of a foreign gerbil and, if the stale smell gets on your gerbils, may cause them to bicker or fight.

Wooden items only need to be washed if they smell; air-dry the wet wood for a few hours before returning it to the tank. Since gerbils gnaw on these, you may want to use only scalding hot water (no bleach) on wooden toys. You can also clean your gerbils' water bottle and food dish in the dishwasher once a month.

# Gerbil Proofing and Gerbil Escapes

If you allow your gerbils to run free, first gerbil-proof the play area to avoid accidents. Remove hazardous chemicals and houseplants, lock up aspirin or other drugs, unplug electrical cords, and block off any gerbil-size holes (for example, the shop vacuum hose). Pick up any clothing, as your gerbil may not only ruin it but ingest thread or get the thread wound around a paw. Make sure that cats cannot gain access to the room.

If your gerbil decides to take an unauthorized free run and escapes from his housing, start an active search the moment you notice he's missing. Gerbils are easier to find than you might think. When napping, they usually sleep in a closet, behind furniture, or in a box. If awake, they often race right around the room. Before the search begins, quickly gerbil-proof the area. Remove cats and dogs to another area of the house, close doors to confine the gerbil to one room, and remove any chemical or

Before allowing gerbils to run free (or if they escape) remove all gerbil hazards: gerbil accessible hiding spots such as a vacuum hose, cleansers, drugs, cloth, wires, cables, electric cords, plants, and especially cats.

electrical hazards. Then do a systematic room-by-room search. Beginning with the room your gerbil started in, look in every possible gerbil-size, accessible place. When you're finished searching that room, close the door and move on to the next room. From my experience, I can tell you you'll probably find your gerbil in the room where he started, and you'll likely find him in less than a half-hour.

If your gerbil is lost and separated from his cage mate for more than twenty-four hours, the scent memory for each other will likely be lost—so don't place him back into the tank with the other gerbil right away. They may fight. Reintroduce them using the split cage method described in Chapter 3.

# Let's Eat! (and Drink)

Wild gerbils eat the leaves, stems, and roots of plants; they also eat seeds, grains, and bugs. Your gerbil will eat similar foods,

There are many healthful treats for gerbils. Give small gerbil-sized portions so that they are able to clean their plates in a sitting (and food doesn't rot).

including oats, millet, seeds, some wheat, and nuts. Whole corn, except for the heart, is filler, so don't waste money on prepackaged gerbil foods containing a lot of corn kernels. Some people feed mealworms or protein-loaded crickets, though live food isn't necessary. Alfalfa or soymeal are other good sources of protein. Gerbils enjoy bits of dried vegetables, like carrots and split peas, in the mix. Most quality commercial gerbil foods provide all the nutrients a gerbil needs, so vitamin supplements are not necessary.

The recommended protein level for gerbils varies widely. Many laboratory gerbils are kept on standard rodent blocks (soy and other grains, seeds, and fish meal, ground and formed into very hard 1-inch pellets), which provide high amounts of protein (16 to 22 percent). Often, commercial gerbil food mixes have a much lower protein amount of 12 percent (the protein percentage is listed on the back of the bag). Studies show that growing gerbils need at least 16 percent protein and develop more slowly with any less, while adult gerbils need about 14 percent protein. Older gerbils can have less (12 percent), if they appear to be slowing down and gaining weight.

If you like a food mix, but the protein level is low, mix it with a high-protein food, such as small animal pellets, lab blocks (you may want to break these into smaller pieces), dry ferret kibble, dry cat food, Kashi or other whole-grain cereal, or peanuts. (Mazuri makes a high-protein gerbil food that contains soybean meal.)

The fat level should be at about 7 percent. If your gerbils seem to be gaining too much weight, feed less food or remove most of the sunflower and pumpkin seeds, which are high in fat. Some lab blocks have only 3 percent fat—but since this is too low for gerbils, you should include peanuts, sunflower seeds, or other high-fat additives. Another reason to supplement lab blocks is to provide stimulation. Though lab blocks may contain all the nutrients gerbils need, gerbils clearly enjoy variety in their food; feeding time is one of the day's highlights. So give them a little commercial gerbil mix or treats in addition to the lab blocks. If you feed them from a ceramic bowl or hanging hopper, scatter some of the seed around the tank, because gerbils enjoy foraging for food.

Do not overfeed your gerbils! They may regulate the total amount of food they eat—but not the *kind* of food. In fact, if they're being overfed, they will search for and eat the high-fat goodies and leave the uneaten high-protein, low-fat pellets and grains. A small handful of food every day is all that two gerbils need.

A common misconception is that gerbils can go without water. Although they each drink only about a teaspoon of water a day and use the liquid efficiently, they always must have access to a water bottle. If they don't drink every day, they will become dehydrated. A 4-ounce, rather than 8-ounce, water bottle is a good size for gerbils. Because the bottle sits higher in the tank, it is less likely to leak from having litter piled up against the spout. A 4-ounce water bottle will provide a seven- to ten-day supply of water for two gerbils. However, it is healthier for the gerbils if you dump out the old water, wash the water bottle, and refill it with fresh water every few days.

Though gerbils are especially fond of treats, these should make up no more than 10 percent of their diet. Gerbils love fresh vegetables and fruit, such as carrots, celery, cucumbers, peas, string beans, apples, grapes, and pears. It is important to wash all fruits and vegetables well, since gerbils can be poisoned by pesticides. Or, better yet, give them organic produce that is grown without pesticides.

Give one tiny (1/4-inch square) bit at a time to each gerbil. Or give them a whole carrot or half-apple to enjoy and then remove it after a half-hour. The problem with giving too many small pieces of fresh produce is that the gerbils will hide them, and the produce may rot. Introduce new types of fresh vegetables and fruits slowly into your gerbils' diet and give only as an occasional extra; otherwise, they may cause diarrhea, especially produce that is high in water content.

Some food treats, such as nuts, give healthier benefits if they are raw; they lose nutrients when roasted. Other foods, such as carrots, are healthier when steamed rather than raw. Sugar is bad for gerbils' teeth and is hard for them to digest, so sugar-sweetened treats, honey, and even dried fruit, should be avoided. Vegetables high in nitrates, such as spinach and lettuce, if fed to gerbils, should be only a very occasional treat (because high levels of nitrates interfere with transportation of oxygen in red blood cells). There are mixed reviews on broccoli and cauliflower; many owners feed these to their gerbils without a problem, but others think you should

Though a gerbil drinks only about a teaspoon of water a day, he needs constant access to his water bottle to prevent dehydration.

Feed a pair of gerbils about two heaping tablespoons of food a day. Scatter some of the mix on top of the bedding to satisfy their natural desire to forage for food.

avoid feeding the "gassy" vegetables. Avoid giving citrus fruits, such as oranges, and carbonated drinks. Chocolate, alcohol, tobacco, some houseplants, onion, and garlic are harmful for many pets, including gerbils. Do not feed uncooked (raw) potatoes and raw beans; some types are poisonous to gerbils.

If you feed from a ceramic dish, your gerbils will bury it unless it is on a ledge. Before you feed them, dig up the bowl to see what is left. The remaining food is likely to be the healthier pellets, seeds, and grains. If there is a lot of food left in the bowl, you might want to skip a day or start feeding less. When food is given directly on the bedding, gerbils create a food store that can be seen against the aquarium glass. By checking this, you can see how much and what kinds of food are left to be consumed.

# Healthful Gerbil Treats

| | | |
|---|---|---|
| Almonds | Kashi or Puffed Kashi cereal | Potato (only if cooked!) |
| Bananas | Kitty/pet grass | Pumpkin seeds |
| Blueberries (fresh or frozen) | Millet spray | Raisins |
| Bread sticks | Natural yogurt | Rice (raw or cooked) |
| Cherrios | Oatmeal (raw or cooked) | Rice Krispies |
| Corn Flakes | Parsley | Sunflower seeds (unsalted) |
| Corn taco shells | Pasta (raw or cooked) | Sweet potato (cooked) |
| Dandelion greens (washed) | Peanuts (unsalted) | Toast |
| Flax seeds | Peas (raw, cooked, or dried split) | Walnuts |
| Hard dog biscuits | Plain croutons | Wheat germ |
| Hemp seeds | Popped plain popcorn | Whole-grain bread |

# 5

# Taming and Handling Your Gerbils

Secure in his owner's arms, a spotted black gerbil takes a moment to pause and pose for the camera.

GERBILS ARE CURIOUS AND OUTGOING BY NATURE AND, as long as you move at their pace, are eager to become your friends. After you bring your gerbils home, observe them to gauge how they feel and when they are ready to start getting to know you. Some gerbils settle right in, running busily around the tank. Others will first retreat to the nest box because they need a little more time in their new environment. Once your gerbils are comfortable in their new home, you can begin working with them. Several short, positive sessions throughout the day (only a few minutes each), rather than one long session, work best. Gerbils are most active in the early evening or early morning, so these are especially good times to work with them.

The American Gerbil Society recommends that only one person (an adult) in the household handle the gerbils initially. Once the gerbils get used to and enjoy being held by this one person, then the rest of the family, including children, can begin holding them, too.

## Speak Softly and Carry a Carrot Stick

As with most animals, gerbils do best when handled by those who are quiet, calm, and steady. Whenever you walk into the area where your gerbils are housed, it is a good idea to get into the habit of announcing yourself and greeting them. Gerbils have excellent hearing, so your greeting doesn't need to be loud; a softly spoken murmur or special identifying sound will do. They'll get to know you and they won't dive for cover or warn each other with a foot thumping when you suddenly arrive.

Below is a step-by-step process for socializing gerbils to their principal handler (let's say it's you), assuming they are young, fairly tame, and without behavioral problems. (Working with "problem" gerbils will be addressed later in this chapter.) Feel free to skip steps or move quickly through the steps if the gerbils are already tame and jumping into your hand to come out and play.

*Wash your hands.* Before handling gerbils, wash your hands in soap and water or with a waterless liquid hand sanitizer (kept next to the gerbil tank for convenience). Certain smells, such as salt, are appealing to gerbils and you wouldn't want a finger to be confused with a french fry! Conversely, other smells, such as soot, seem to be repugnant to gerbils.

A pretty Siamese takes a pumpkin seed gift. Hand feed pumpkin seeds, sunflower seeds, and other choice morsels when you are getting to know your gerbils.

*Create a safe environment.* Close and, if possible, lock the door to the room in which you'll be handling your new gerbils. This will keep them in and other pets—such as cats, dogs, and ferrets—out. Close all doors and cabinets; make sure any hard-to-reach hiding spaces are blocked off.

*Talk to your gerbils.* Take the top off the tank and speak softly to your gerbils in a mix of words and noises (smooches or clicks, for example). Get their attention. Let them see, hear, and smell you over the top of the tank. Take your time; if either you or they feel anxious, spend several sessions or even days getting to know each other by sound and sight before moving to touch.

*Give gifts.* If they are curious (listening and standing up tall), try offering them a gift, such as a sunflower seed or a small (1-inch) cardboard tube segment. They may snatch it right away, but if not, lay your hand on the floor of the tank and be completely still for a moment; hold the gift and see if they will take it from you. If they won't accept it from your hand, leave the offering in the tank and try again with another gift later. While you are taming your gerbils, give them, by hand, the choice morsels from the food mix, such as, sunflower seeds, pumpkin seeds, and peanuts.

*Linger.* Once your gerbils seem comfortable with having your hand in the tank, remove all the tank accessories, then lay your hand and forearm on the bottom of the tank. Be as still as possible. Let your gerbils sniff, explore, and climb on you. Baby gerbils may still be at the stage where they're putting everything in their mouths, so they may do some exploratory nibbling on your fingers. Either ignore the tickling feeling or let them know that you are not for tasting by saying, "Ouch!" or, "Hey!" or, "No!" If they don't respond to verbal correction, give a quick puff of air in the face (as though you were blowing out one birthday

Once a gerbil is completely comfortable with an adult handler, she can begin getting to know the rest of the family, including children.

candle). Gerbils are very smart and will quickly learn not to nibble on you. No matter what your gerbils do, never jerk your hand away. Keep still or move away in a slow, steady movement; since your gerbils are looking at your arm as a climbing structure, they'll consider you an unstable, rickety one if you make sudden, unpredictable motions!

# Handling Techniques

When handling gerbils, the key is to be steady and firm, without squeezing or gripping them. Holding gerbils tightly probably makes them feel as though they are trapped in the clutches of a bird of prey: they don't like it. Your confidence and steadiness will give them a sense of security. Below are tips for helping your

## How Gerbils View You

**SOME SMALL ANIMALS DON'T LIKE HANDS IN THEIR** cages because they see these as invasions of their territory. This is not true of gerbils. According to world-renowned gerbil expert Julian Barker, you are their territory. Sometimes gerbils will even rub their bellies against you to mark you as their own. As soon as your gerbils start to know and trust you, they'll welcome your arm in the tank as something fun to explore. From my observation, gerbils don't seem to see people as one whole being. Your hands, arms, and shoulders are the stairs, ladders, and platforms that bring them closer to your face, which they relate to as another gerbil. They listen to your utterances, wink at your eyes, and try to reciprocate your kisses.

gerbils take the big step of leaving the security of their home to come out and explore your hands, arms, shoulders, and even head (if you don't mind!). After getting a taste of playing in the outside world, most gerbils will be eager for more.

## The Elevator Ride

When one of your gerbils is sitting in your hand for more than a millisecond, try lifting your hand straight up, very slowly, all the while murmuring pleasing sounds. She'll probably leap off, so lower your hand to the floor of the tank and try again. And again. And again. And again. Eventually, you'll be able to lift her 6 inches or more off the floor of the tank. At that point, you don't want her jumping off and getting hurt. So, with a steady motion, move your hand up more quickly to draw her out of the tank and up against your body.

You may feel the gerbil vibrating in your hands; this means she's purring and content. After a few minutes, put your gerbil

Gerbils quickly become uncomfortable or frustrated when held still. Notice that this gerbil is holding the ears back to indicate his displeasure.

When holding a gerbil, keep your hands still and steady without constraining the gerbil's movement.

back into her house and rest your hand and arm on the tank floor again. Since gerbils learn by watching each other, once one gerbil learns the trick of sitting in your hand for an elevator ride, the other will follow. After a while, your gerbils might become impatient with the slow elevator service and decide to take the stairs— that is, scramble right up your arm and onto your shoulder!

## Boxes, Scoops, and Tubes

If your gerbils seem uncomfortable with the elevator ride, try to gently but confidently pick them up a different way. Again, don't grab or squeeze and don't handle them in a hesitant or timid manner; these behaviors make gerbils uneasy.

There are two methods for picking up a gerbil. One easy method is holding a small box (around 6 inches) on the bottom of the tank, with the opening on the side, not top, of the box. Almost immediately, one or both of your gerbils will jump into it. When only one gerbil is inside, with a steady movement that's

A one-handed grab is like being snatched by a bird of prey to a gerbil. Do not do this when picking up your gerbil.

To pick up a gerbil, scoop from the front and underneath using two hands.

not too slow, tilt the box and lift it up. Pour the gerbil into your hand. Let her explore your hands and arms for a short time (30 seconds), and then return her to her tank.

Another method is scooping her out with two hands. It is important not to hover one hand over your gerbil or to reach down from above. From a gerbil's perspective, this looks like an owl's claw swooping down to grab her. Instead, place both hands palm up on the bottom of the tank and slowly herd one gerbil into a corner. In a fast but smooth, steady motion, scoop her up by cupping your hands under and around her. Then, lift her up. If she seems relaxed during this movement, repeat it several times a day. If she seems nervous or jumpy, then revert to letting your hand linger in her housing near her for a few sessions before scooping her out again.

Suppose your gerbil somehow gets out of your hands and onto the floor? There are two ways to pick her up. Rest a close-ended tube or box on the ground, which most gerbils cannot resist exploring, and lift it (and her) up as soon as she crawls inside. Or, alternatively, watch where she is going and make a corral with both your hands about 10 inches ahead of her. Then, quickly scoop up your gerbil as she's running into your hands.

# Reasons for Nipping or Biting

Gerbils are gentle animals that handle stress well. When well socialized to humans and properly handled, they'll seldom bite. So, what accounts for those rare occurrences when they do bite? And what should you do if your gerbils nip or bite? In order to answer these questions, let's begin by defining three terms: mouthing, nipping, and biting.

*Mouthing* is exploratory behavior, usually by young pups. Baby gerbils are still in the stage where they put everything in their mouths, so they'll gently explore objects and people by using their mouths and tongues to feel them. Mouthing doesn't hurt, it tickles. It is nothing to worry about and is behavior gerbils will outgrow.

*Nipping* may or may not hurt. Usually the skin is not broken, although a nip may sometimes leave a small nick. When your gerbil nips, she actually is using restraint and is more interested in communicating with you than in hurting you. The most common reason a gerbil develops a nipping habit is as a response to unsteady, timid, or rough handling. If a gerbil is handled roughly—startled, grabbed, squeezed, swung, or dropped—she may be forgiving at first but, over time, will react by nipping. If you pop your gerbil back into her tank after she nips you, she'll quickly learn that her nips are a signal to you that she's had enough. Eventually, your gerbil may decide to skip the rough treatment altogether and nip you as soon as your hand enters her tank. Your gerbil also may nip because there is the scent of salt or food on your hands. Occasionally, a gerbil may go through a personality change after the death of her cage mate; she may become nervous and irritable and nip until she is paired with a new friend.

If your gerbil nips you, tell her to stop it (use a "No!" or "Ouch!") and blow a quick puff of air into her face. Though she may be anxious to get back into her home, wait ten seconds before returning her to the tank. Otherwise, she may interpret this as a reward for nipping you. Above all, respect what the gerbil is trying to tell you with her teeth and stop doing whatever you're doing when she nips.

*Biting* occurs when the gerbil chomps without restraint. Your gerbil may even hang on, dangling from your finger for a moment. Do not panic; remain calm and assure her that everything is okay. She should then let go, thus preventing a severe bite. A gerbil bite typically produces two small, deep punctures. Be sure to clean them well to prevent infection. If swelling occurs or if you have any other concerns, call your physician, especially if you do not have a current tetanus shot.

There are a number of situations in which a gerbil may bite. The most common instance is when a gerbil is touched while fighting another gerbil. (This is an automatic response; take the appropriate precautions before placing your hand between squabbling gerbils.) Additionally, a lack of socialization to humans may cause your gerbil to nip or bite. She also may bite due to repeated rough handling that continues even though she has given warning nips. This may happen, for example, when an unsupervised child plays roughly with a gerbil and ignores her attempts to communicate distress by nipping successively harder. Finally, nipping or biting might occur because a gerbil is in severe pain. If a normally sweet-tempered gerbil bites without provocation when picked up, there is a good possibility that she needs medical treatment.

## Taming "Problem" Gerbils

Keeping gerbils that nip or bite when you first bring them home is not recommended for those new to gerbils. If you are able to return these gerbils to the breeder or pet store, consider doing so and then search elsewhere for a well-bred, well-socialized, tame, and friendly pair.

If you decide to keep a pair that nips, try working through the taming steps outlined in this chapter—but do it very slowly. It's important to act confidently, even if you have to fake it. One trick when taming "problem" gerbils is to focus on the friendlier of the two and ignore the other one completely. Gerbils learn from observing one another. If one gerbil sees the other climbing onto your hand and up your arm with no ill effects, she is likely to follow. If your gerbils have been mistreated or mishandled in the past, you may discover that they are afraid of hands. They may be happy to come see you and play if the dreaded hand is covered by a sleeve. In time, hand-avoidant gerbils may be okay with a closed fist and perhaps, someday, they'll even accept a finger scratch behind the ears.

A tamed and trusting gerbil is a beautiful thing.

# 6

# Gerbil Health and Hazards

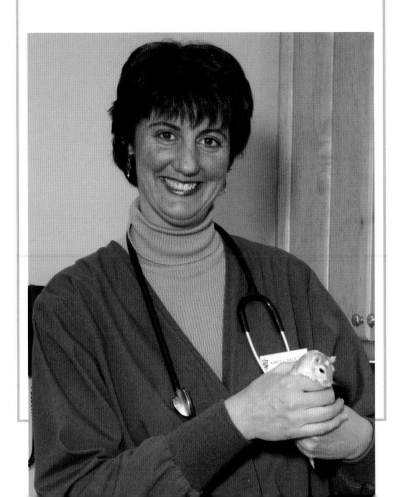

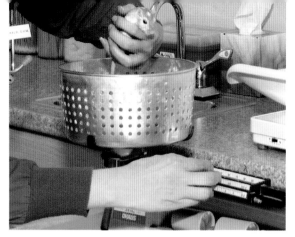

The vet weighs the gerbil to see if he's lost weight and to mix a proper gerbil-sized dose of oral medication.

GERBILS ARE HARDY AND HEALTHY ANIMALS WITH FEW associated health problems; your gerbils most likely will never become ill or injured. But, in case something should happen, since prevention and rapid intervention in the early stages of any illness are critical, you want to be able to identify common health problems. In addition to illness and injury, other potential situations that may arise include poisoning, parasites, aging, and eventually death.

The information provided in this chapter is intended as an aid to understanding gerbil ailments. It is not, however, a substitute for qualified veterinary care.

# Ounce of Prevention

By far, the biggest danger to gerbils is improper care. Your gerbils need to live in a clean, dry, and stimulating environment and be given a constant supply of healthful food and clean water. The good news is that care-related problems are completely preventable by exercising some simple precautions and by making a daily check on the gerbil tank. Knowing your gerbils' typical appearance and behavior is the first step toward preventive care.

Healthy gerbils have smooth, shiny fur (not puffed). A gerbil with greasy fur may simply need a chinchilla dust bath (see sidebar). Healthy gerbils are active and easily shift from sleeping to being awake and playing. Their eyes are bright, shiny, and wide open. The nose is not red or runny. They should not click, sneeze, wheeze, or have labored breathing. Their bottom and underside should be clean and dry and their poop should be firm and dark. A healthy gerbil will investigate any new object in the tank and grab the choicest pieces when fed. Danger signs for a gerbil include listlessness, loss of appetite, or rapid weight loss or gain. A normally friendly gerbil who doesn't want to leave the

## Chinchilla Dust Baths

**THOUGH NOT AN ABSOLUTE NECESSITY, WEEKLY CHINCHILLA dust baths are great fun for gerbils and leave their coats soft, sleek, and shiny. Put two to three tablespoons of chinchilla dust into a shallow bowl and place it in the gerbil tank. Your gerbils will roll, flip, fluff, and dig into it. Throw it away after a half hour, before your gerbils kick it out of the bowl or start using it for a potty.**

# GOOD HEALTH CHECKLIST

√ **Smooth, shiny fur**
√ **Fur not puffed**
√ **Active**
√ **Easily awakened**
√ **Playful**
√ **Bright eyes, shiny and wide open**
√ **Nose is not red or runny**
√ **Does not click, sneeze, wheeze**
√ **No labored breathing**
√ **Bottom and under** _____ **d dry**
√ **Healthy stools**
√ **Curious**
√ **Good appeti**
√ **Normal a**
√ **Usual fr**

Do a quick health check every day. With proper care, your gerbil should live a long, healthy life.

tank and even nips or bites when touched is likely to be ill or injured and in pain. Keep a close eye on your gerbils and, if you see any changes, call your vet.

# Pound of Cure

Without the proper treatment, gerbils can go from healthy to sick to dying in a matter of days.

Since time may be critical if your gerbil falls ill, you should have on hand a gerbil medical emergency kit containing the following items:

- Phone numbers for a small-animal vet and animal poison center

- Eyedropper or infant medicine dispenser or needleless syringe (from a pharmacist)

- Ornacycline antibiotic (go to the bird section of a pet store or find it online); use the dose for a small bird

- Neosporin (from the drugstore) for slight cuts and wounds

- Reptile lamp, desk lamp with adjustable neck, or clamp lamp

- Reptile lightbulb or 40-watt grow bulb

- Stick-on aquarium thermometer for the outside of the tank

- Hot-water bottle that can be filled with either hot or cold water, depending on the situation

- Corn syrup (mixed with equal part warm water) to hydrate or revive a gerbil

## Allergies

A red, runny nose with no other symptoms is probably an allergy rather than an illness. The most common allergies are to certain types of litter. For example, cedar and pine contain harmful oils

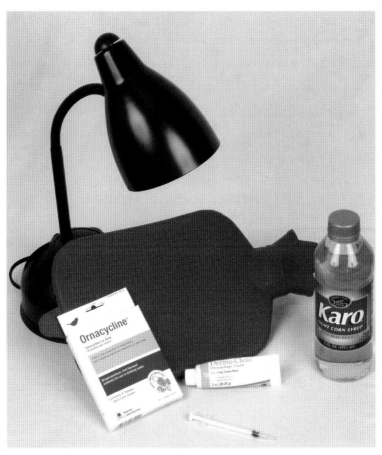

Time may be of the essence when treating an ill or injured gerbil, so keep a medical emergency kit on hand.

that can cause not only allergies but also liver damage and other ailments. Owners often confuse a runny nose with a bloody nose, since a gerbil's mucus is a brick-red color.

If you think your gerbil has an allergy, try changing his litter to another type. If his nose does not clear up immediately, it may be an infection that responds to Neosporin. If the problem persists for more than a few days or other symptoms are present, call your vet.

## Broken Limbs and Head Injury

A gerbil that falls from a great height onto a hard surface may have broken a bone, usually a hind leg. A clean break will heal on its own without medical treatment. However, if the injury is to the head, the gerbil may roll uncontrollably. Keep him warm and call a vet immediately. A gerbil with a severe head or back injury may have to be euthanized. (If you have a jumpy gerbil, the best way to avoid these injuries is to sit while holding him or to hold him over a blanket, rug, or other soft surface.)

## Broken, Misaligned, or Overgrown Teeth

If a gerbil is not eating and seems to be losing weight, check his teeth. If they are misaligned or overgrown, have your vet trim them (or show you how). If the front teeth are broken or missing, feed your gerbil soft foods, such as cooked oatmeal, applesauce, baby food (or cooked and mashed) vegetables until the teeth grow back.

## Dehydration

It is important to check the water bottle daily to see that it still contains water and is working correctly. The signs of dehydration initially may be subtle. In early stages, thirsty gerbils may be more active than usual or may be quarrelsome. Later on, the gerbils may look thin or feel lighter when held. They may have puffed, rumpled-looking fur, and their eyes may be half-closed and dull. With severe dehydration, gerbils may sleep a lot.

If your gerbil is dehydrated, provide a working water bottle and a high-liquid fruit or vegetable. In extreme cases, mix warm water with an equal amount of corn syrup and feed with an eye-dropper. Call your veterinarian.

## Detached Tail and Degloving

A gerbil should never be held or grabbed by the tail. A gerbil's tail is detachable in the middle and it could come off in your hand. If this happens, don't worry. You are likely to be much more upset over it than your gerbil is. Put a little Neosporin on the tip of the remaining tail. It should be fine, but if it gets infected, contact your veterinarian. Unfortunately, the tail will not grow back.

Degloving is a similar injury in which the tail, usually just the tip, is skinned, leaving muscle exposed. The exposed tail should dry out and, in a few days, drop off. If the tail becomes infected or doesn't fall off on its own, consult your vet; it may need to be amputated.

This beautiful Agouti's tail was accidentally pulled off by a pet sitter. Make sure everyone who handles your gerbils knows "Hands off Tails."

## Diarrhea

Diarrhea in an otherwise healthy gerbil might be caused by a gerbil's diet. If you are feeding him greens or a lot of fresh fruit and watery vegetables, stop these until your gerbil's diarrhea stops. Then, give these foods only in moderation. Be cautioned, however, that diarrhea can be a sign of a very serious illness, especially when seen in combination with other symptoms. So, keep a close eye on your gerbil and call your vet if you don't think his diarrhea is diet-related or if your gerbil doesn't immediately improve after a change in diet.

## Heat Stroke

If they have deep litter and a nest box, adult gerbils can tolerate temperatures ranging between 65 and 84 degrees, though they will begin to show effects of the heat at about 77 degrees. Babies are more sensitive to the heat and cold and should be kept in temperatures ranging between 71 and 75 degrees.

A sign of gerbil heat stroke is inactivity. In the early stages of it, your gerbils may stretch out on a smooth surface and pant. In the more advanced stages, they may be unconscious and wet around the mouth.

If your gerbils are in the early stages of heat stroke, simply move the tank away from the sun and to a cooler part of the house, such as the basement. Usually, the floor is the coolest area of a room. Put a refrigerated stone in the tank. Offer cool water or a vegetable that has been soaked in cold water.

If the problem is more advanced—for example, your gerbils are unconscious—you must gradually bring down their body temperatures. You could put your gerbils on a hot-water bottle that is filled with cold water, use a bag of frozen food wrapped up in a towel, or cool a small room (such as a bathroom) with air conditioning. Don't blow cold air directly onto your gerbils. When your gerbils regain consciousness, offer a drink of cool water. If they don't drink on their own, try giving them one drop of water at a time with an eyedropper. Bring your gerbils to the vet as soon as possible, as they may need an injection of fluids.

## Hypothermia

Hypothermia in gerbils can be caused by exposure to very low temperatures or by the animal's being wet for a long time (from several hours to days). Signs of gerbil hypothermia include feeling cold to the touch, inactivity, huddling together in a tight ball, and nonresponsiveness to sound or your touch.

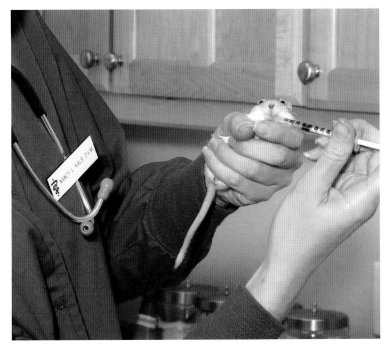

Ask the vet to show you how to give your gerbil liquid medicine. The dropper is inserted to the side of the mouth behind the front teeth.

If you see signs of hypothermia, call your veterinarian. In the meantime, gradually warm your gerbils. For example, use a heating pad under half the tank (so the gerbils can move off the heat once they are revived). You can also use a hot-water bottle filled with very warm water—or heat a small room (such as a bathroom) with a space heater. You could try placing the gerbils against your body under your clothing. The temperature around them should rise to a range of 77 to 85 degrees. Once your gerbils are revived (and this may take an hour or more), give them a drink of water.

## Inner Ear Cyst and Infection

If an older gerbil has a permanent head tilt, it is likely caused by cholesteatoma, an inner ear growth. Though untreatable, the gerbil usually continues to function well. A more serious secondary condition—namely, an inner ear infection—can make the gerbil lose balance, circle, and hold the head at a strange angle. This infection is treatable by a veterinarian, who uses an anti-inflammatory injection coupled with oral antibiotics. If the inner ear infection goes untreated, the gerbil will become incapacitated and die.

Another type of head tilt, accompanied by swaying, is due simply to a ruby-eyed gerbil's trying to focus his vision. This is nothing to worry about.

## Kinked Tail and Fixed Wrist

There are very few genetic defects associated with gerbils. Two that are sometimes seen and are present from birth are a bend in the tail or wrist. Both are minor issues. They will not prevent your gerbil from living a long, full, active, and healthy life.

However, such a gerbil should not be bred, as this trait can be passed to the offspring.

## Mites

Mites are an annoying parasite that can be hard to get rid of, especially if you have numerous small animals that become infested. Usually, mites arrive on their host animal, namely the gerbil. But they can be introduced from food or bedding or even come home on your hands or clothes if you handle infested animals at a pet store or gerbil kennel. As a precaution, some owners will freeze their gerbils' seed mix to kill any mites and their eggs.

Mites are slow-moving red or black dots, about the size of a pinhead, that pop blood when you squash them. Everything exposed to mites and their eggs must be treated for six weeks. The most successful way to get rid of live mites and their eggs is by following a total treatment plan.

To treat your gerbils, spray them down to the skin with bird mite spray every week. (Caution: this could poison a frail or baby gerbil! Wash it off immediately if your gerbil has a bad reaction.) Be careful not to get the spray in their eyes; as an alternative, you may want to wet a paper towel and rub the spray into their fur. In addition to mite spray, an oral treatment of Ivermecin every two weeks for a total of six weeks is very effective; this is a nonprescription drug, but you'll need your vet to mix the proper dosage for your gerbils.

Any open bedding, food, or items made of wood should be thrown away. Hard plastic, glass, and metal can be run through the dishwasher, submerged in boiling water, or washed in scalding hot water with a few drops of bleach and then rinsed well in very hot water. Spray the rims and covers of the tank with bird

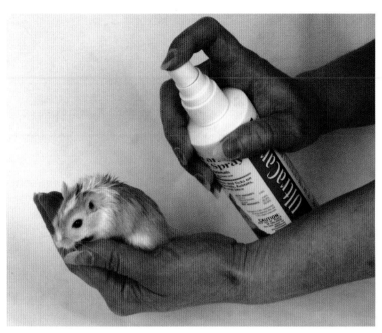

Like most gerbils, this spotted Argente (being sprayed for mites) is surprisingly tolerant of treatment. When giving treatment, sweet talk your gerbil and don't constrain him for too long without giving a short break to stretch his legs.

mite spray. Stronger sprays and medications are available from a vet, if you have difficulty getting rid of these pests.

Spray indoor bug spray (and wipe dry) on the shelving that holds their housing and on hard floors surrounding it (but not inside the gerbil tank). On your rugs, spread and immediately vacuum flea powder made for carpeting. When you are done treating the gerbils and their supplies, use laundry detergent and hot water to wash your clothes. To kill mites on you, use Head & Shoulders dandruff shampoo on your hair and as a body wash.

## Ovarian Cyst and Scent Gland Tumor

Though the condition is uncommon, an older female gerbil may develop an ovarian cyst. This is a growth in the ovaries that, though not life-threatening, can become quite large. Your female gerbil may eventually look pregnant or it may appear that she has swallowed a golf ball. Though these are inoperable, I have seen and heard of cases where a large cyst will rupture and simply disappear.

Some male gerbils develop a tumor on the scent gland. Since a scent gland tumor grows outside of the body, it can be surgically removed by a qualified veterinarian. The success rate is high, especially when the gerbil is not too old and the tumor has not progressed for too long.

## Poisoning

Gerbils are sensitive to poisons. Household chemicals, cleaners, and flea powder can be fatal if a loose gerbil runs in an area where these substances are present. Even mite spray made for small animals, though safe for an otherwise healthy, adult gerbil, can poison a frail or baby gerbil. Pesticides on fruit or vegetables also can be poisonous to gerbils.

A gerbil that is poisoned may shiver or shake or may just seem to be rapidly fading away in front of your eyes. If your gerbil gets poison on his skin, act quickly. Immediately wash or dip him in warm water. Once he is revived, dry him (e.g., with paper towels and by having him take a dust bath) and keep him warm.

Gerbils also are vulnerable to poison in the air. Like canaries that used to be brought into the mines to detect harmful carbon monoxide levels, gerbils will faint or expire if even a low amount of this gas is in the air. If you think poison is leaking into the air, everyone in the house (including the gerbils and other pets) should be removed from the residence. Call the fire department and then call the animal poison control center or your own veterinarian for treatment of your pets.

## Respiratory Infection

Signs of respiratory infection include clicking sounds and labored breathing. Sick gerbils may also have puffed fur and dull, half-closed eyes and feel cold to the touch. In adult gerbils, cold-like symptoms may progress to a respiratory infection if left untreated. Baby gerbils are especially vulnerable to respiratory infection during weaning.

A respiratory infection must be treated immediately; if left untreated, it can kill your gerbil. If you suspect respiratory infection and cannot see a vet right away, treat the entire tank of gerbils with Ornacycline (sold for birds), using the dose for a small bird, for a full 10 days. Keep the gerbils in a clean, low-dust environment (consider switching to corncob litter and using unscented toilet tissues for bedding). Warm only one corner of the tank to 80 degrees and use a thermometer to monitor the temperature.

## Seizures

Seizures or fits are brought on when a gerbil who is prone to them is overwhelmed or scared. With a mild seizure, a gerbil will lie still and then freeze for a period of time (from a few seconds to a few minutes). With a more severe seizure, the gerbil may first shake or twitch and then freeze. If your gerbil has a seizure, put him back in the tank and talk softly to him or turn down the lights and leave him alone.

Gerbil seizures should not be cause for alarm. They are not life threatening or serious; they do not cause brain or other long-term damage; and many gerbils who have seizures as pups will outgrow them if they are handled frequently and gently. A gerbil who has seizures may be more sensitive to loud noise, being grabbed, and crowds of people—so handle him with care.

## Preparing for the Unexpected

**AS A PRECAUTION, SHOULD A SNOWSTORM, HURRICANE,** *or other emergency take place, the American Gerbil Society recommends always keeping an extra gerbil water bottle and a week's supply of litter, gerbil food, and fresh water on hand.*

## Strokes

A gerbil, especially an older one, who appears weak or paralyzed on one side or who has difficulty walking may have had a stroke. A gerbil may have multiple strokes and die from them, but gerbils are also known to survive strokes and to recover from most or all of the paralysis caused by them. If your gerbil has had a stroke, keep him warm and comfortable with access to food and water. Lower the water bottle and put plenty of food in his reach. If he's having trouble holding seeds in his paws, try hand-feeding him soft foods like cooked oatmeal and baby food. Strokes do not need medical treatment, but the symptoms are similar to an inner ear infection, which does. So, call your veterinarian if you are unsure whether your gerbil has had a stroke or suffers from an inner ear infection.

## Tyzzers

*Tyzzers* is a word that sends shivers through the gerbil enthusiast because it is a horrible disease that will wipe out an entire gerbil clan. Tyzzers is caused by a bacterium called *Clostridium piliformis* and creates symptoms of listlessness, watery diarrhea, and rapid decline. It can cause death. There is no known cure, but if you put your gerbils on antibiotics and keep their stress levels low, you may keep your gerbils asymptomatic for some time. Tyzzers is transmitted to healthy gerbils through direct contact with infected gerbils or through exposure to their litter or bedding. It is important that new gerbils come from a reliable source and undergo a two-week quarantine before being introduced into a gerbil kennel.

If you're a breeder and your gerbils contract Tyzzers, you must discontinue any breeding and you should not place your infected gerbils into new homes.

# Aging

Like a fine wine, gerbils get better with age. Older gerbils have a special sweetness about them and become completely self-assured. With age, they will have honed their skills at charming you so you'll take them out, or they may insist upon it by climbing up your arm during your daily water bottle check. Once out, they may even sit with you for a bit before going off to explore and play. Older gerbils may have a lighter, faded coat, and some

Many older male gerbils, like this three-year-old boy, take an immediate liking to young pups. You may want to get two babies so the youngsters will have each other once he passes. Some females will accept a new friend, though others prefer to be alone.

colors lose their ticking (black fur tips). But, most gerbils will remain healthy and active to the end.

As a gerbil approaches the end of his life, you may see his coat getting dull, and he may take frequent, long naps and be harder to wake. He may not keep his eyes open fully. One day, you may find him motionless but breathing deeply. Most gerbils die peacefully and from old age; they are likely to die quietly, often in your hands, as you murmur your final good-bye. However, if your gerbil is unable to enjoy a minimal quality of life or is in pain, as a final kindness to him, you should have him euthanized.

## Saying Good-bye

In a world that doesn't always understand or value the companionship provided by small animals, it can be hard to mourn the loss of a gerbil friend. Though many may be sympathetic over a friend's loss of a dog or cat, they may scoff over sadness expressed when a pet gerbil dies.

What can you do? Finding a special burial place, such as a spot in a park or in the woods where two trees cross, helps some people say good-bye. Others create a formal gravesite and marker. Talk about how you feel to those who knew your gerbils or who have had a personal relationship with their own pets. Find a reputable online E-list (check the site's archive before joining any list!), such as those moderated by the American Gerbil Society or National Gerbil Society, to share memories of your gerbil friend with others. There are Web sites dedicated to gerbil memorials, such as a special American Gerbil Society online page, where you can post a picture, story, or poem.

Perhaps the best healing is a visit with another gerbil. If you still have a gerbil at home, spend extra time with him; giving him exercise, especially free runs, will help him cope better with living alone. If he's willing, introduce him to another gerbil friend, using a split cage (Chapter 3). An elderly male might accept two pups, and the youngsters will have each other when he passes. When you are ready, visit pet stores or local breeders just to look. Maybe two fortunate little gerbils will charm their way into your heart and home.

If an older gerbil is left without a companion, spend extra time with him and if he seems lonely (lethargic or irritable) consider finding him a new gerbil companion. (Free runs are a lone gerbil's antidepressant.)

When the time comes to welcome new gerbils into your home, look for ones as healthy as this pair.

# 7

# Breeding and Raising Gerbils

A litter with eyes opened held in two hands is a rare sight. This litter is accustomed to photo shoots. One baby is even settling down to wash her face.

THERE ARE MANY THINGS TO CONSIDER BEFORE DECIDING to breed gerbils. Before bringing any new gerbils into the world, you should have adoptive homes lined up for them or commit to keeping them yourself for their entire lives. Without careful planning—and at the rate one pair of gerbils procreates (about six pups a month; well over a hundred in a lifetime)—what you envisioned as a fun hobby can quickly become a burden. In order to anticipate all that is involved, ask yourself these questions:

- Realistically, do I have the necessary time and freedom to commit to breeding gerbils?
- How many babies can I afford to keep and adequately care for?
- Is there a market in my area for gerbils? (If there are many local pet stores, this indicates a good small-animal demand.)

- Do my children and I have the stomach for dealing with still-born gerbil pups or other young gerbils who may die?

- Do I have the resources to find homes for the babies (money for extra equipment and advertising, space for nursery tanks, time to screen and educate potential buyers, transportation to bring them to new homes or to the pet store)?

- How will we feel when the time comes to give up some of our babies?

## Unplanned Parenthood

When planning for gerbil pups, preparation is recommended to make the experience enjoyable and successful. However, gerbils frequently decide to have pups without bothering to consult with you first. What should you do if a surprise litter appears in your tank?

First, take a deep breath! This happens all the time: either one of the gerbils advertised as a "male" is female, or one or both of your females became pregnant in the pet store (which happens if a female older than seven to eight weeks is housed with an adult male).

Second, sex your gerbils yourself (see Chapter 3). If you have two females, leave the mother and pups in the original housing setup and move the other one into a separate tank. (If you are not sure which gerbil is the mom, watch for the one who is nursing and has babies attached to her nipples for a second or two after she leaves the nest.) Two mature females in a breeding environment make a stressful and volatile combination. They may get along at first, but then, without warning, one may injure or kill the other, or even attack the pups.

Alternatively, if you have a female and a male, keep them together to raise the pups. Gerbils mate during or immediately

Sometimes a pair of gerbils have a surprise litter, as above. Both male and female gerbils are almost always great parents, but two females together are a volatile combination with pups in the mix.

after birthing. So, by the time you discover the newborns, it will be too late to prevent the next litter—your mama gerbil is already pregnant! A female can become agitated over the removal of her mate and, without him, might neglect her pups. As a bonus, male gerbils are wonderful fathers. In addition to keeping the babies warm, grooming them, and stimulating their bathroom functions, the dad provides the mother gerbil warmth, security, and much-needed full-body massages. Gerbils are usually great at parenting, so give the new mom and dad some privacy to let their instincts for raising babies kick in.

You should remove from the cage any serious hazards to the newborns, such as a high tower or perch. Then, don't change anything else. The loss of a beloved item in the tank could distract the parents from caring for the babies and cause them to spend hours fussing over it and trying to put their house back in order.

# PlannedParenthood

If you decide to plan a litter, your first step is to select a breeding pair. If possible, work with a breeder so you can see the health, temperament, and parenting skills of the gerbil line. These are all important considerations, as these traits are passed to the off-spring. Below are some questions to ask the breeder:

- What is the fatality rate of past litters, including deaths from stillborns, illness, or injury? (A fatality rate under 10 percent is excellent.)

- Are the parents in this breeding line attentive and nurturing to the pups from newborn through weaning stages? (Any injuries inflicted by the parents should signal a red flag. Don't breed from these lines.)

- Have there been runts or any pups in the litters with respiratory infection?

- Have there been any genetic defects or issues in the lines, such as kinked tail, fixed wrist, or seizures?

While health and temperament come first, breeding for color is important, too. Producing the more in-demand colors and color variety can help later, when placing the pups. (It may also increase your own enthusiasm for breeding.) The breeder can help you pick gerbils who will produce the colors you want; you may be able to get pedigrees showing lineage and genetics of your new breeding pair. Certain colors, such as ruby-eyed white or Agouti, can be harder to place, especially if the entire litter is composed of one of these colors. Owners usually want the fancy colors and they want two gerbils they can tell apart. Spotted gerbils tend to be popular in any color. There are many online

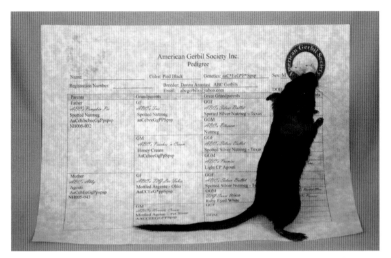

A black female gerbil examines the pedigree of a potential pied black male mate. Knowing the genetics of your breeding pair allows you to predict the colors of the babies they will produce.

resources that explain gerbil genetics, and these sources can help you figure out what colors a particular breeding might produce.

If there are no gerbil breeders close to you, find an unrelated breeding pair by obtaining male and female gerbils from two pet stores that are located far from each other. A brother and sister or parent and offspring can and will mate, but I wouldn't recommend these pairings. Too many generations of inbreeding (mating of close relatives) might produce pups with health or temperament problems.

## Setting Up House

After you have selected your breeding pair, introduce them gradually and carefully (as described in Chapter 3). Once your gerbils are a happy couple, create a home and atmosphere that are conducive to breeding and rearing a family. While candlelit dinners and romantic music are probably not necessary, you do want to

A simple breeding tank with a towel draped over one side removes hazards and encourages the mother to focus on the babies. Make sure to hang the water bottle low once the babies are about two weeks old so that they can reach it to take a drink.

establish a safe and low-stress environment for them to get started on—and raise—a family.

An aquarium is recommended over a wire cage, since the pups could wiggle through or get stuck between bars; a glass tank also will protect the pups from drafts. Place the breeding tank in a warm, quiet, and calm location in the house. It is good to expose the babies to a low level of noise, but too much activity and sound (especially loud, sudden noises) can cause stress. Make sure it is an area safe from little hands (and big paws). Pick a spot for the housing and set up the breeding tank well before the babies are birthed to allow the parents time to settle in.

When breeding, the gerbils' housing should be kept simple, without levels, ladders, tubes, or towers. Remove anything that may crush or suffocate a pup. You can drape a towel over half of the tank to create a "den" without posing any potential danger to the pups. Provide 3 inches of litter and lots of unscented toilet tissue for them to nest and hide in. Cardboard bits with a short chew life can be given to the parents when the babies are tiny and need constant attention; these bits will satisfy the parent's desire to gnaw without distracting them for too long or posing a suffocation hazard to the babies. Small, lightweight boxes and tubes can be introduced starting when the babies are three weeks old.

Clean the tank about a week before the babies are due to be born because, once the pups are birthed, you should not change anything, even if the tank was not recently cleaned! Wait two or three weeks before cleaning out the tank again. If it starts to smell, replace the litter in just one corner of the tank each day; don't disturb the nesting corner where the newborn babies are. The one exception to the rule is wet litter: make sure to remove it immediately. Finally, before the pups arrive, put together an emergency birthing kit (see sidebar).

Pups sometimes need special weaning foods to help them transition from nursing to eating on their own. They are also susceptible to respiratory infection, which is treated with Ornacycline or other antibiotic and a heat lamp in one corner of the tank for warmth.

# Gerbil Birthing Kit

## HERE'S WHAT YOUR GERBIL BIRTHING KIT SHOULD CONTAIN:

- Clamp lamp and reptile warming light or 40-watt grow light
- Stick-on thermometer (for the outside of the tank)
- Powdered kitten milk replacement
- Eyedropper or infant medicine dispenser
- Ornacycline antibiotic (sold for birds; found in pet stores or online)
- Emergency contact information for a vet and other local gerbil breeders

## Mating

If both gerbils in your breeding pair are youngsters, they may not mate until they are three months or older. However, an adult male or female, especially an experienced adult, may mate at the first opportunity, even if paired with a gerbil as young as seven or eight weeks old. Sexually mature female gerbils are receptive for breeding every four days.

Female gerbils produce pups until they are nearly two years old, and sometimes older, although the litters are likely to be smaller and farther apart with an older female. While many other types of small animals have age-related issues like pelvic hardening, and must be bred early, this is not so with gerbils. A female gerbil can have a first litter at any age, though you'll have better luck introducing a female to her mate if she's young.

You may or may not observe your gerbils mating. Usually, they mate in the early evening for about a two-hour period. It is pretty much a G-rated affair of chase and tag (where the male

A pregnant female is fat only in the belly area, giving her a pear-like shape.

mounts for only a second), and then each gerbil peeks at his or her own underside. If you do witness the mating behavior, mark your calendars. The babies will arrive on or about twenty-four days later. When a gerbil is nursing a litter, the gestation is delayed and the mother gerbil will remain pregnant for up to five weeks, maybe longer, before the new litter arrives.

## Caring for the Mom-to-Be

Gerbil mothers will be active and energetic right up to (and often including) the birthing of the pups. Except for giving extra protein, little special care is needed. Make sure to feed her a high-quality gerbil food, with 18 to 22 percent protein. You can boost the protein by feeding her dry kitten food, ferret kibble, chicken-laying feed, peanuts, an all-natural multigrain cereal such as Kashi, or bits of scrambled egg. (Scrambled egg should be fed in a ceramic bowl, and you should make sure to remove whatever is not eaten after a few minutes so it doesn't rot.)

Now that she'll be eating for seven (or so), give the mom-to-be plenty of healthful food and as much of it as she wants. It is critical during pregnancy and while nursing that a constant water supply is available for the mother gerbil. Dehydration is the one reason a mother gerbil will consume a pup: if necessary for survival, she will use the pup as a source of liquid. So check every morning and evening that the water bottle hasn't run dry and that it is working properly.

A few days before the birthing, the mother gerbil starts "showing." If she is carrying a large litter, she may appear pear-shaped or look like she's swallowed a Ping-Pong ball. If you take her out of the tank in the last days of pregnancy, handle her carefully to make sure she doesn't fall.

# Birthing

Often, gerbil pups are born at night or in the early morning hours, though they might be delivered any time. If you see the pups being birthed, either leave the room or watch very quietly from a distance. A first-time mother may be nervous, and it is important not to distract her from her task at hand. During birthing, the mother gerbil will reach down between her hind legs and pull out the pup; she'll break the sack and eat all of the birthing material, including the placenta, which is rich in protein. Then, she'll clean off the pup.

Some mothers place the pups in one neat pile; others may have the babies scattered during the birthing. The male and female may work on creating the next litter between deliveries or immediately after the whole litter is birthed. If there are older pups still in the tank, they are often curious about their new

This mother gerbil is nursing newborns while the father stands guard and protects them.

siblings; they may groom them or just run over them. The birthing tends to have more of a party atmosphere than that in a hospital maternity ward!

A couple hours later, all should be calm and quiet. The mother gerbil will create a large nest in one corner, gather up all the pups, and retreat inside the nest to nurse. The newborn gerbil pups will peep softly like baby birds. The father gerbil will settle in another corner, away from the family nest. He and his mate are not arguing; evidence suggests that newborn male pups emit a high level of testosterone, which adult male gerbils find unpleasant. Thus, Mom is left alone for the first twenty-four to forty-eight hours to nurse the babies and to bond with them. After a day or two, the dad will return to the family nest.

If the parents seem distracted and are not attentive to the pups, try giving them unscented toilet tissue for nesting, draping a towel over one half of the housing, turning down the lights, and leaving them alone for as long as possible. Occasionally, one newborn will become separated from the rest or a lonely dad will steal a pup for company. In either case, return the pup to the mom. *Note:* It is extremely important to wash your hands or wear a plastic baggie on your hand before touching the newborn! Your gerbil knows you and your smell, but if a strange smell gets on the pup, the mother could reject or attack him. These foreign smells include soot or smoke, other gerbils (outside their clan), and stale gerbil litter (never reuse old litter, even their own).

## Fostering

It's common for a first litter to be smaller than the average litter size, which is six. Having only two or three pups is a good way to ease gerbils into parenthood. If a single live gerbil is born, however, this is a problem. Typically, a single pup cannot stimulate enough milk flow and starves, despite all of the mother gerbil's efforts (and yours).

If a single pup is born, the best course of action is to foster her with another litter of gerbils. The younger the litter, the better. Mother gerbils are very accommodating about taking in a foster pup, as long as the pup is under a week old and not yet furred. A furred pup, on the other hand, smells like an unfamiliar gerbil, and a would-be foster mother gerbil will quickly kill her.

Fostering is easy if you follow these simple steps:

- Wash your hands.
- Remove from their tank the parents that are getting the foster pup.

If a gerbil pup needs help in weaning, tilt her back slightly and teach her to lick kitten milk replacer from an eyedropper by putting a tiny drop on her lips. Never force feed a gerbil.

- Take the pup to be fostered from her nest and immediately place her underneath the pile of baby gerbils so she doesn't get chilled.

- Wait five minutes and put the dad gerbil back in the tank. (He'll likely discover and groom the pup.)

- After five more minutes, return the mother gerbil to the tank to examine and nurse the new member of the family.

## How Gerbils Grow

Gerbils grow up quickly, so enjoy them as they change before your eyes! Gerbil pups are born blind, deaf, and naked, and are completely dependent upon their parents. Even though their eyes are closed, the skin is so thin that you can see whether they will have black eyes (these are dark splotches under the skin) or ruby eyes (these blend into the skin color). In the first days, you will even be able to see the white milk in their bellies, so you'll know they are being well-fed.

After a few days, the skin pigment indicates whether you will have dark- or light-furred pups and you'll notice any spotting patterns. Gerbils will grow little walrus-like whiskers and tiny toenails, and their ears will open.

When the pups are a week old, you can start handling them (see sidebar). Unlike hamsters, which become easily stressed when raising a litter, gerbils are usually fine having you handle their offspring, as long as you wash your hands first. When you take the pups out of the tank, they will crawl around enthusiastically for about three minutes, then fall asleep in a gerbil pile, each trying to dig her way to the bottom to keep warm. When they are a little bit older, they will wash their tiny whiskers and face before napping in your hands.

Newborn gerbils are blind, deaf, and furless. They peep softly like baby birds in the first week or so.

This 10-day-old Burmese pup is already very relaxed being handled. It is important to always wash your hands before touching baby gerbils.

You will be able to determine the genders of the pups at seven to ten days, by checking which have nipples. Nipples are present only on female gerbils; at this age, they appear as dents in the upper thighs, sides of the belly, and arm pits. If the pups are different colors or have distinguishing spotting, write down this information, along with the gender of each gerbil. This way, you can advertise and take reservations on the same-sexed pairs. After ten days, the pups' bellies become so furry that the nipple dents don't show. You won't be able to sex the gerbils again until they are five weeks, when the male and female parts become noticeable and distinguishable.

From ten to nineteen days, the gerbils grow a nice thick coat of fur, but the eyes are still closed. Though they

Besides being unbelievably cute, eating Cheerios is a good way to help these baby gerbils wean from their mother's milk.

are blind, if you handle them at least a few times a week, the pups will come to know you by your touch, taste, and smell. They'll explore your sleeves, lick your fingers, and sit right in your hand as they give themselves a thorough grooming.

At or about nineteen days, the pups open their eyes. Sometimes the eyes open only a crack and you might not even realize they have their vision except by their strange behavior. In the first few days after gerbils open their eyes, they may race around the tank at top speed, jump at any new sound or sight, and suddenly seem terrified of you.

It is important to continue handling the pups at this stage. Just be careful! Take them out one at a time, cupped in two hands. You may not be able to hold them with open hands for a couple of days; be prepared to have them take off like a shot if you do. Hold them down low and only in a confined space. The pups are simply overwhelmed by the bright lights and visual simulation, and you look like a looming giant! In two or three days, the pups will come to recognize you by sight, and once again enjoy visiting with you. At three weeks they look and behave just like miniature versions of their parents.

# Weaning and Separating the Pups

Between two and three weeks of age, the pups will begin nibbling on food. In addition to regular gerbil mix, they enjoy softer weaning foods such as Cheerios, peeled sunflower seeds, and canary seeds. (There is nothing cuter than a three-week-old gerbil holding a "giant" Cheerio in her paws!) Though they are eating solid food, they continue nursing, too, until somewhere between four and five weeks. And, don't forget the water! It is important that the water bottle is low enough for the pups to

## Safe Pup Handling

**CAUTION! WEEK-OLD BABY GERBILS MAY BE BLIND,** but they are surprisingly fast. If you drop them from any height, permanent brain damage may result. Follow these safety precautions when handling them:

- Always wash your hands before touching the gerbil pups.

- Lay a clean towel, pillow, or blanket on the floor.

- Give the parents some food or treats and a few inches of paper towel roll to keep them busy. Keep an eye on the parents' reactions. Occasionally, Mom or Dad (especially first-timers) will be nervous about the pups' being handled.

- Take out the pups, completely enclosed in your two hands.

- Rest your hands on the towel or pillow before opening them.

- Don't keep week-old pups out for more than a few minutes.

- While completely enclosed in two hands, return them to the nest; don't open your hands until they are resting on the floor of the tank.

reach. If you see that one or more of the babies are licking the side of the tank, spray the glass with water droplets until they discover the water bottle.

Natural yogurt is healthful weaning food and can be fed with cooked oatmeal and baby food (mashed apple, banana, or carrots) to weanlings (three to five weeks old) who need an extra push or have been rejected or lost their mother. Growing gerbils need a high protein level of at least 16 percent.

The pups can be moved to a nursery tank at five weeks—or sooner if a new litter arrives before then. At this age, pups should be held gently and frequently so they develop into tame, people-loving little companions. The American Gerbil Society recom-

This baby gerbil will follow his dad's tame behavior, so don't separate them too soon.

mends waiting until the pups turn six weeks old before placing them in new homes. Female and male pups should be separated at seven weeks to prevent any chance of their mating.

# Limited Breeding

Though gerbil breeding pairs develop a strong bond, lifetime mating is sometimes not feasible. Limited breeding is possible, but it only works with young female gerbils (six months or younger), as they are more adaptable than older females to changes in their family structure. If you must stop breeding an older, established pair, speak to your vet about the possibility of neutering the male so you can keep the two gerbils together.

You can try this method for limited breeding: Put together an unrelated male and female pup. They'll grow up together, mate at about three months, birth pups at about four months, and together raise a litter. Since gerbils mate while or shortly after birthing a litter, the female will be pregnant with a second litter. Wait to remove Dad until the first litter is weaned, but

# Problems During Weaning

**DURING WEANING, GERBIL PUPS ARE ESPECIALLY**
*vulnerable to respiratory infection. Act immediately if the babies start to make clicking noises, especially if they also have labored breathing, feel cold to the touch, have puffed fur, or are slowing down or have stalled in growth. Treat the entire family, including the parents, with an antibiotic. Ornacycline is a gerbil-safe antibiotic that is available over the counter and found in the bird section of a pet store or online (have this on hand if you are breeding). Use the dose prescribed for a small bird or parakeet, and place the medicated water in the gerbils' water bottle; the medicine needs to be replaced every day. Several times a day, place a few drops directly onto the lips of any pup showing symptoms. Treat for a full ten days. If necessary, you can obtain a stronger, prescription antibiotic from your vet.*

*If any of the pups seem to be weak, or if their development slows, make one corner of the tank warmer (no higher than 80 degrees). (Use a stick-on thermometer outside the tank to help regulate the temperature.) Supplement their feed with kitten milk replacement. (Buy the powdered type and mix a teaspoon at a time.) Let the baby lap the milk from an eyedropper a few times a day. Don't mix the kitten milk with the medicated water, as it will lessen the antibiotic's effectiveness. Give kitten milk and antibiotic at least one hour apart.*

before the second one arrives. A few days before this litter turns five weeks (or sooner, if the mother looks like she's getting heavy in the midsection), put Dad and the sons into their own tank. Let Mom and one or two daughters raise the next and final litter.

Another option is to contact local gerbil breeders (the American Gerbil Society has a breeder listing). Find a breeder who is retiring a young breeding female and is willing to give you a pregnant mom and a five-week-old daughter who will raise one litter of pups together.

# 8

# Fun with Gerbils

Gerbils like to play inside and pop out from a sleeve "tunnel".

THERE ARE MANY WAYS TO HAVE FUN WITH GERBILS. A simple, homemade toy is appreciated by them. You can also have your gerbils make something for you, such as a paper snowflake. Another fun activity is photographing your gerbils; tips are provided below that will allow you to capture their cuteness without wasting a lot of film. Your gerbil is more than a pretty face; he is intelligent, too. If you understand how to motivate your gerbils, you can even teach them to perform tricks.

## Entertaining Your Gerbils

Gerbils are easily entertained by any item that satisfies their desires to gnaw, build, burrow, climb, and run. If you've had a demanding day, it is nice to come home to two little furry-faced friends who take great pleasure in the smallest gift. Here are a dozen simple ways to entertain your gerbils that are guaranteed to put smiles on their faces:

- Open up the gerbil tank cover, peek in and click, whisper, smooch, and coo at the gerbils. Tell them how cute and nice they are. Hum a song. "Twinkle, Twinkle Little Star" is one of my gerbils' favorites.

- Hand-feed them some pumpkin or sunflower seeds, or give them each a peanut in the shell.

- Toss an empty paper towel roll into the tank; to a gerbil, it doesn't get much better than this!

- Give them a big handful of alfalfa or timothy hay. It has a similar effect as catnip on a kitten and will make your gerbils extra frisky.

- Rest your arm in the tank and let them explore you; even better, do so wearing long, loose sleeves they can climb inside.

- Build stairs by fastening together two or three different-size boxes with Elmer's glue. Cut some holes in the sides of the stairs. Use masking tape to attach the stairs to the side of the tank.

- Divide the tank with an 8-inch cardboard "fence"; they'll have fun getting over, under, and through it.

- Nab a clean, processed-cardboard drink holder from a fast food restaurant and partially bury it in the litter.

- Give them a tissue box with one-fourth of the tissues still in the box (be sure to remove the plastic cellophane lining). Make sure the tissues are unscented and without lotion.

- Make a sandbox (filled with playground sand) or put a bit of chinchilla dust in a glass jar that is resting on its side.

- Crumple a large paper bag and wedge it in the tank to create a gerbil rock-climbing wall.

- Gerbil-proof a new area and let them run free: this is Gerbil Utopia!

# Gerbil Art Projects

Gerbils love receiving gifts, but they also enjoy giving them. I love it when my gerbils make me snowflakes. It's an easy activity: Simply fold a square or circle shaped piece of paper into symmetrical folds and give it to them. However, don't walk away from the tank, or your snowflake may "melt" completely! When a quarter of the paper is gnawed, remove and unfold it to find a unique snowflake design made of tiny gerbil nibbles.

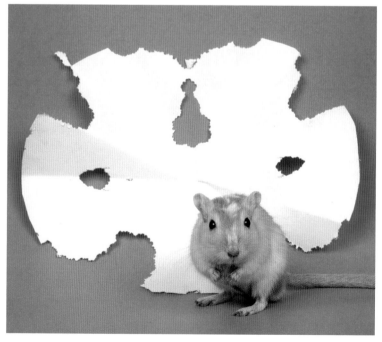

Buzz, a mottled Argente, is a champion chewer always willing to create snowflake art.

How about letting your gerbil run through some non-toxic poster paint to design gerbil paw-print note cards? (When he's done, have him run through ¼ inch of warm water and then let him take a dust bath to clean off his feet.)

If your gerbil seems to have an artistic bent, you could even let him try his hand (actually, his teeth) at sculpting. One famous gerbil named Phoebe was the companion of New York City artist Judith H. Block and lived in an apartment surrounded by books, paintings, and classical music. Rather than simply gnawing tubes into a new layer of litter, Phoebe would sculpt them. She would chew, pause, observe her work, and then chew some more in a particular spot; she would then move to another area, creating the definite shapes of an abstract sculpture. Phoebe's work has been exhibited at gerbil shows and can be seen at www.phoebe.agsgerbils.org.

# Photographing your Gerbils

Maybe your gerbil's talent is as a gerbil model. Gerbils are extremely photogenic because of their natural curiosity and cuteness. However, there are tricks involved in taking pictures of gerbils; without them, you are likely to end up with lots of blurry shots of a furry gerbil buzzing by.

The key to photographing gerbils is to provide a nice background and perhaps some props in a limited area. Props can be used to show perspective (e.g., a playing card) or to alter the perspective (e.g., a "giant" gerbil next to a toy model of the Empire State Building). Confine the area where your gerbil can roam to only 1 or 2 feet. Either you can have someone else place the gerbil into the prop and then take the picture as soon as the gerbil is released—or you can use a confined area and wait until the gerbils explore the

To take an adorable family photo like this, create a gerbil photo studio using a small table, box, white sheet, and nest box.

prop. Focus the camera on the entire area and wait for the cuteness to occur. Then snap.

Try capturing these pictures: a gerbil holding a Cheerio in two paws; a gerbil emerging out of a tube; gerbils sitting on a dollhouse chair or couch; or a gerbil pup in a toy crib or carriage. A picture of a gerbil in front of a bright-colored construction paper background makes a professional looking photograph. To celebrate a holiday, photograph your gerbils as they investigate a classic symbol, such as a Halloween jack-o-lantern.

The biggest challenge is capturing pictures of gerbils in groups. There is something about a camera that makes gerbils scatter. But, there are ways to take a group photo. One method involves using a bottomless nest box. When the gerbils are sleeping in the nest box, quietly take the cover off the tank. Focus the camera on the bottom of the nest box and then have someone else lift it in the air. You'll have three to five seconds to capture a pile of sleepy gerbils before they disperse.

Here is another trick for photographing a group of gerbils (again, getting this shot takes two people): Put a cute, hollow ceramic with a bottom (such as, a ceramic strawberry) in one corner of the tank. When the gerbils are napping in it, take out the ceramic filled with sleepy gerbils. Have your helper hold it about 3 feet in the air or place the ceramic so it is right on the edge of a table (in either case, make sure the gerbils are over a pillow, just in case someone gets camera shy and leaps) and then snap a picture of the gerbils as they peer out over the edge.

If you have a digital camera and are able to crop pictures, you can take a shot through the aquarium and cut out the area where the flash hits the glass. Placing the tank in natural lighting and taking a picture without the flash works, too. If the tank has just been cleaned out, your gerbils will be very busy, providing the opportunity to photograph them engaged in their various gerbil activities.

Ruby-eyed gerbils photograph better in natural light, as a flash will cause "red eye." Place your gerbil "studio" several feet in front of an open window on a bright day. With your back facing the window, take the pictures without a flash. If you have to use a flash, wait until your ruby-eyed gerbils are not looking directly into the camera. The camera's red-eye-reduction feature will help some, but the delay might cause you to lose your shot.

# Training Your Gerbils

Can gerbils be trained? Yes! You can train your gerbils using positive rewards and negative results. Below are step-by-step instruc-

Cardboard tube, boxes, and some masking tape make a great gerbil playground.

tions on teaching several tricks that are especially suited for gerbils. But first, it's important to understand how gerbils learn and what motivates them to perform.

In one respect, gerbils are among the easiest animals to train, because they will teach each other. In fact, with very little exposure, gerbils within a tank will copy behaviors. It is extremely cute to see a mother gerbil crawling up your arm and onto your shoulder with four or five babies following in a line.

Gerbils will even learn behaviors by observing gerbils in other tanks! For example, I once brought home a new gerbil who would spring straight up in the air in an attempt to knock off the tank top. Soon my other gerbils in tanks throughout the gerbil room were leaping in the air and bumping their heads on their tank covers; obviously, they were copying this behavior. If one of your gerbils seems smarter, more outgoing, and more confident than the other, you can focus your training on that one and let the other pick up the tricks from him.

## Motivation

There are three keys to training a gerbil:

- Choose a behavior that your gerbil does (or could do) naturally.

- Assign a visual prop or sound cue (not word) for the trick.

- Reward the behavior the moment it occurs.

Whereas most trainable animals, such as dogs and rats, are motivated by food or being petted, these are not especially good rewards for a gerbil. Though in limited circumstances, food rewards will work (for example, for a simple trick such as "beg"). It is important that while you train them with food rewards your gerbils be in the tank, as the excitement of being out of the tank makes most gerbils indifferent to the tastiest treat.

Better than food, the most effective reward, especially for physically or mentally challenging tricks, is "out time," when they can explore and run. The trick should either logically end in time outside of the tank or, once the trick occurs, the gerbil should be immediately taken out of the tank for a run. When the run is over, make sure to give your gerbil some playtime on you and cardboard in the tank. If you simply pop him back in his cage he'll dodge away from you the next time your try to catch him.

Although soft pleasing sounds are not the primary motivators, gerbils do appreciate hearing these sounds, such as cooing, clicking, and smooching, when they are making progress learning a trick or have successfully completed one.

Now, here are some tricks you can teach your gerbils.

## Stay Put

To stop an undesirable behavior—for example, leaping off a table—use a harsh (but not loud) sound, such as "awk, "hey," or "no" when the gerbil even considers doing it (say, he begins to peer over the side of the table). Your gerbil will respond by stopping whatever he is doing and looking at you. After a few repetitions, he will stop attempting the behavior. You can use this technique, for example, to have your gerbil stay put for a photo shoot. A gerbil who doesn't listen after a few "awks" goes back in the tank for a short time; eventually, he'll learn to "stay put."

## Come

"Come" is a practical trick to teach, especially if you have a complicated housing setup with tubes, levels, and ladders that makes it hard to get at your gerbils. Build a platform at the top of the tank or next to the door of the cage where you can easily access the gerbils. Start by using food to teach this trick; the best time is when your gerbils are hungry. (Though not as good a motivator as "out time," hungry gerbils when inside their housing do respond to getting treats.) Evening before being fed is ideal because the gerbils will be both hungry and active. The signal for "come" is a sound cue, such as two quick taps on the rim of the tank. Make the signal and then leave two sunflower or pumpkin seeds on the platform (it's okay if the gerbils don't get them right away). Keep doing this several times in an evening, over a period of days, until the gerbils approach the platform when they hear the taps. At this point, change the reward. When they near the platform, take them out of the tank or provide a ramp exit and immediately let them run free in a confined space, such as a desk top, a bathroom, or a bathtub lined with a towel. Let them play for a few minutes and then put them back in the tank. Once they are off the platform, double tap again and reward their coming with another free-run session. Soon your gerbils will be racing up to the platform as soon as they hear the signal to "come out and play."

## Beg

"Beg" is an easy trick to teach. This is one that can be taught with food rewards, so teach this trick when your gerbils are hungry (right before you feed them). To teach them to "beg," use your fingers in a pinched shape as the signal to your gerbils for this trick. Start by holding a sunflower or pumpkin seed between your fingers pointing straight down at about 2 inches above the floor of the tank. The gerbils will come over and take the treat. Gradually, over a period of days, lift the treats higher and higher until the gerbils have to stand

The best reward for a trick well down is getting to come out to play.

very straight and tall to get the treat. When you want to show off the trick, use just the signal (pinched fingers over their heads).

## Hit a Punching Bag

Once your gerbil knows "beg," teach "hit a punching bag" by holding a tiny gerbil-size bag between your pinched fingers (as usual, pointing down just over the gerbil's head height). When the gerbil comes up for the seed and hits the bag, immediately drop a sunflower seed or two. He'll soon learn that swatting at the bag will dispense seeds his way.

## Shoulder Ride

Some gerbils are natural-born shoulder riders, but even if it doesn't come naturally, any gerbil should be able to perch on your shoulder for a bit. Put him on your shoulder and if he tries to climb down say, "awk" or "hey." If he climbs off, put him back. At first, have him stay for only ten seconds. Gradually increase the time until he stays for a few minutes. When he can balance on your shoulder, try walking. Some gerbils enjoy shoulder rides and that is reward enough. Others will do it only for a bigger prize. Release your gerbil with a sound such as "yay!" or by patting your chest. Then, let him climb down and have a run.

## Leap into a Hand

To be taught to jump into your hand, a gerbil must first be tame and able to crawl into your hand and up your arm as described in Chapter 4. When your gerbil climbs out onto your arm, allow him to play on you for a few minutes, or give him a short free run. When you put your gerbil back home, he'll be highly motivated for more out time. Lift your hand, palm held open and parallel to

A spotted Burmese named Thunder demonstrates the shoulder ride balancing on his haunches.

the ground, just a half-inch off the floor of the tank. Make sure to hold your hand steady. Over time, increase the height in half-inch increments until your gerbil is leaping up to 8 inches or even higher to get into the palm of your hand.

## Run a Maze

Gerbils are superb at memorizing paths, and will run a maze if given the right incentive. A gerbil maze should be made of tubes—for example, PVC pipes—rather than being open at the top (he'll simply leap out of this type of maze). The diameter of the tubes must be large enough for your gerbil to turn around. Your maze should end in an open tube and result in freedom. To start off, take your gerbil out of the tank and put him inside a straight, open-ended tube. Then, start adding bends and dead ends. Time your gerbil to see how fast he can run the mazes. As with all supplies, wash the maze pieces between uses.

# 9

# Exhibiting Your Gerbils

Though all wild gerbils are Agouti, this natural-looking gold-and-black brindled nutmeg poses in a exhibit showing the type of grassy plains where wild gerbils live.

NOW THAT YOU'VE BEEN CHARMED BY GERBILS, PERHAPS you want to show them off to the outside world. There are many opportunities for exhibiting your gerbils. You can create an exhibit for your local library, support a humane society educational event, or visit an elementary school. You can even have your gerbils compete in a virtual gerbil show or in a live, sanctioned match.

## Gerbil Exhibits

Schools and local libraries often welcome gerbils as visitors or for permanent display. If you are interested in creating an exhibit featuring your gerbils, try replicating the look of wild gerbils living in their native habitat. (Two little wild-colored Agoutis will add further realism.) To do this, fill the bottom of a 20-gallon-long tank with 1/2 inch of sand covered by a few inches of corncob. Make one corner a sandbox (or chinchilla dust bath area). Partially bury a kiln-dried branch (available from pet suppliers) so the gerbils can climb on it or tunnel through the "roots." Add a clump of grasses (alpha or timothy are sold in bundles at pet stores) every few days. If you are a creative type, try building a visible underground tunnel and chamber against the front side of the tank, using clear tubes and a small plastic carrying cage. Insert a picture or drawing of the Mongolian plain as the back wall and accompany the exhibit with photographs of and a short write-up about Mongolia and gerbils in the wild.

Volunteering to support an animal rescue event or pet expo provides another opportunity to exhibit your gerbils. Put together a 10-gallon-tank housing setup within a certain budget (e.g., $40) and show your two gerbils enjoying it; beside that tank, place an exhibit of what not to do when owning gerbils, and feature a ceramic gerbil rather than a real one. Challenge spectators to find the five things that are wrong with this "picture"; for example, show your little ceramic gerbil all by herself (gerbils should be kept in pairs), in a 5-gallon tank (they need more space), with an open-slat wheel (a tail could get caught), cedar litter (it's too harsh), and no tank lid (she'd jump out). You could offer stickers, a certificate, or a ticket in a drawing for anyone who gets all five answers correct. The American Gerbil Society offers a free, downloadable, two-sided gerbil care brochure, which anyone is allowed and encouraged to print out and distribute. This is a nice take-away handout you could offer to visitors when manning an exhibit or making an educational presentation.

# Gerbil Presentations

Gerbil visitors are a huge hit at the elementary school level; a tank of gerbils usually attracts about thirty children in as many seconds. For a highly visual and experiential presentation that is sure to please, follow these steps:

*Preparation*: Ahead of time, gather a water bottle, food, treats, paper towel roll (tunnel), sand, chinchilla dust in a bowl, alpha or timothy hay, a wooden nest box, a wheel, cardboard boxes of various sizes, litter, and unscented toilet tissue. Hide these supplies in a bag. Put your gerbils in a 10-gallon tank containing nothing except 1 inch of bedding. Cover the tank with a towel. Bring the covered tank and the bag of items into the classroom.

*Introduction*: Start the presentation by asking who knows what a gerbil is, who's had gerbils, who knows what a hamster is, who's had hamsters (make it clear that you are talking about the big "regular" Syrian hamsters and not the dwarf ones). Tell the children that you are going to show them gerbils and that you want them to observe the way they look and act. Now, take off the towel covering the gerbil tank. The gerbils will have been in a low-stimulation environment and so likely will be standing up in a corner pressed together, nervous but curious.

*Questions and Answers*: Can the students tell you the three ways gerbils are different from hamsters? Have the children make guesses until they give all three: (1) gerbils have tails, (2) gerbils are awake during the day, and (3) gerbils live in pairs. If necessary, give them hints, such as: what is your hamster doing right now? (Sleeping.) Next, explain that this is not a very good home for gerbils because gerbils need certain things to keep them safe,

healthy, and happy, and these gerbils look hungry, nervous, and bored. Have the children guess what gerbils need. If they make a correct guess, then put that item (hidden inside the bag) into the tank. The gerbils will go from anxious and still to excited and active as they explore each new item. If the students are stumped, give a hint about where gerbils live in the wild and how they behave; for example, "Gerbils live in a sandy prairie and dig underground tunnels." You might want to make up a list beforehand of hints for each of the items.

*Conclusion and Follow-up:* At the end of the presentation, give each child a certificate as a "trained gerbil

Gerbils are active in the day and exhibit a wide variety of behaviors. This student uses a tally sheet to make scientific observations and record the frequency of behaviors—such as eating, drinking, grooming, digging, standing up tall, thumping hind feet, resting, and sleeping.

caregiver." You may also want to leave the gerbils in the classroom for a couple of days. This will let the children see a wider range of behaviors, including how gerbils dig tunnels and chew cardboard into substrate. Consider posting a tally sheet next to the tank that lists common gerbil behaviors (grooming, eating, sleeping, burrowing, etc.) and having the children record their scientific observations.

## Gerbil Shows

Showing your gerbils is simple, inexpensive, and a lot of fun. At a gerbil show you meet people who share your enthusiasm for gerbils and who love chatting about them as you much as you do. You see firsthand many gerbil colors that you may have seen only in pictures. You learn about the gerbil standards, colors, and genetics, as well as about good practices for husbandry and breeding. You may even win ribbons and points towards a championship and, someday, come home with the ultimate prize: the Best in Show rosette.

Gerbil shows have long been popular in the United Kingdom with numerous regional shows a year, and now they are gaining popularity in the United States. The American Gerbil Society holds live, sanctioned shows every year, as well as fun, virtual matches online. In addition, some 4-H groups and rodent clubs use the American Gerbil Society standards for judging gerbils at their small-animal events.

## Gerbil Show Standards

Before deciding to take the plunge into showing gerbils, read the American Gerbil Society or National Gerbil Society show standards and understand what a show-quality gerbil looks like in

MOTTLED
CLASS

The American Gerbil Society

A judge examines the head of the gerbil and marks a scoring sheet. This judge is working alone, but often a teenager who is interested in becoming a judge someday will assist.

terms of body type, coat, and coloring. Once you feel able to recognize an outstanding gerbil, visit several pet stores, shelters, and breeders until you find mature gerbils that match the standards. Another way to acquire a show-quality gerbil is to attend a gerbil show. While there, find a breeder who has champion or winning gerbils, and make arrangements with the breeder to purchase gerbil pups from that line. At a gerbil show, some breeders will sell gerbils who have just won ribbons in their class. Remember: no gerbil is perfect, so a slight flaw should not prevent you from acquiring and showing an otherwise magnificent animal.

The overall appearance of the show gerbil should be one of a beautiful animal in her prime who has a nice build and symmetry, a healthy and shiny coat, good coloring, and a friendly, outgoing personality. Conformation of the gerbil is 50 percent of the score. A male gerbil must be muscular and bulky—think of the gerbil equivalent of a football player, rather than a runner. (Male gerbils usually do not mature into their full masculine build until eight to ten months of age.) Female gerbils, on the other hand, must look athletic yet streamlined. (A feminine appearance in a male or vice versa is a major fault.) Other desirable physical traits in the show gerbil include a small-broad (not mousy) head; small ears; bright, almond-shaped eyes; and a thick tail with a large, full tuft of hair on the tip.

Color accounts for another 25 percent of show scoring. Each recognized color has a specific color standard for fur, whiskers, eyes, tail, and even toenails. Whatever the hue, coloring should be vibrant and rich, rather than faded or dull. Some colors, such as nutmeg, must have an undercoat in one color and either light or heavy "ticking" (fur tips) in another. Other colors, such as black, should be uniform all over, including whiskers and

A show gerbil, such as this Red Fox, has brilliant color and a soft, shiny coat. A male show gerbil must have a firm, decidedly masculine build.

toenails. Most "self" gerbils (colored belly) in the United States have some white on the throat or paws; this is a fault that show enthusiasts are trying to breed out. A self gerbil without any white markings or stray white hairs is striking.

Temperament determines the final 25 percent. Some other types of small animals are taken out of the show pen with a scoop when shown, placed on a screen, and left untouched during the judging. Not so with gerbils. The judge handles the show gerbil while examining and measuring her against the physical standards. A nervous nip will cost points and probably knock an otherwise top gerbil out of the ribbons. The conformation, coloring, and confidence of a top-winning gerbil combine to give her a flashy appearance that judges sometime call the "wow" effect.

In addition to the conformation judging, there are usually fun events for gerbils and their owners at a gerbil show. If you have gerbils that are not of show quality, you can still enter them in pet classes where they compete on their talent, such as fastest paper-towel-roll gnawer. Gerbil shows generally are kid-friendly events and provide special gerbil-related craft making, coloring, and other activities.

## Getting Ready for the Show

Carefully read the show's Web site, flyer, or other documentation to make sure you are following all of the show's requirements. Participating in an American Gerbil Society–sanctioned match, for example, requires membership in the society and registration of your gerbils. For a sanctioned show, you will probably need to sign up your gerbils in advance, give your membership number and your gerbil's registration number, and pay a small exhibition fee.

Most, if not all, small-animal shows require that your kennel be quarantined prior to the show. This means that no new animals may visit or be introduced into your kennel for a specified period of time. Though gerbils are hardy animals, this is done to ensure they arrive at the show in a healthy state and do not spread parasites or infections to other animals.

Always provide show gerbils with plenty of high-quality food. In the weeks before the show, feeding extra sunflower seeds can add bulk, if needed, and make the fur shiny. (Cut back on fatty foods, though, if your gerbils are overweight.) Provide them with exercise equipment, such as a wheel and a run-around plastic ball, and give them runs outside the tank. Get into the habit of lifting your gerbils out of the tank for a few minutes several times a day to get them used to extra handling. Handle the gerbils as a judge would and examine their teeth, undersides, tails, and other features.

A mottled Burmese show gerbil gets some last minute primping with a good brushing just before judging begins. Preparing a gerbil for the show starts months ahead with exercise and handling.

# Bath Time

**SOME COMPETITORS BATHE THEIR GERBILS TO MAKE** sure they look their best. White gerbils, especially, benefit from having any stains washed out of their fur. Here's how the experts do it:

- Fill two large bowls or sink basins with warm water that is neck-level deep.

- Rub a thin layer of very mild, safe shampoo (such as baby shampoo or kitten shampoo) on your hands.

- Put the gerbil in one basin to get her wet and, when she scrambles into your hands, rub all the shampoo into her fur, on the body only (not on her head).

- Put her back into the basin for a first rinse; rub her fur to lather any remaining soap.

- Then, put her into the second basin for a final rinse.

- Immediately blot your gerbil with paper towels and then dry her thoroughly using a warm light to bask under and a bowl of chinchilla dust to roll in.

When it is time to pack up and go to the show, make sure to bring the entire gerbil family—that is, all gerbils that share the tank or cage of the gerbil you are showing. A gerbil separated from her clan will be stressed, and might not be accepted back into the clan once she returns home. If possible, transport the gerbils in their regular housing setup. Though gerbils tend to travel well regardless, being in their own housing will help keep them happy and relaxed. Purchase a smaller travel tank for them if their regular setup is too large or elaborate. As a courtesy to other exhibitors and spectators, clean out the cage the day before you leave for the show.

A mottled Agouti is placed in her shown pen for judging. Before the pen is placed on the show table, a label is affixed stating the gerbil's age, gender, color, and class. No identifying information (such as gerbil's or owner's name or kennel) is provided so the that the gerbil can be judged fairly.

Bring along a standard-size show pen (12 x 8 x 8 inches) for each gerbil who is competing. (A medium-size Lee Kritter Keeper or a 2-1/2-gallon tank both work well.) Don't place your gerbils in the pen until immediately before the judging begins. Other items to bring include: directions and a phone number for the hotel or show site, clean litter (for the show pen or in case the water bottle drips), extra water bottles, food, carrots or celery, a shallow bowl and chinchilla dust, small cardboard boxes and tubes, and money for specialty gerbil merchandise.

# It's Show Time!

Plan to arrive at the show the night before or early that morning. When you arrive, your gerbils (and any other small animals you bring into the show site) will go through a health check. The health checkers (and judges, too) always disinfect their hands between gerbil handlings to keep from passing on germs. If gerbils appear sick, wounded, or have parasites, they—and any other animals from that gerbil kennel—will not be admitted to the show.

Most exhibitors give their gerbils a chinchilla dust bath immediately before the judging begins. You might do this in their housing and not in their show pen; otherwise, the show pen will look cloudy or dirty from the dust. Some exhibitors use small, soft-bristled brushes to groom their champion hopefuls. Prepare the show pen by placing in it an inch of clean litter, a scrap of cardboard, food, and a clean vegetable such as carrot or celery (do not use wet vegetables such as cucumbers, which make the gerbil's fur appear greasy). Attach the proper identification to the show pen. The show secretary usually provides an ID sticker that states the gerbil's show number, gender, age, and color.

Each gerbil is placed in her own show pen and is put on a table for her category, as follows:

- White belly: non-spotted gerbils with a body color other than white and a white belly (e.g., Agouti)

- Self: the belly matches the body color (e.g., black) or is one shade lighter than the body (e.g., nutmeg)

- Colorpoint: The nose, tail, and paws are darker than the body (e.g., Siamese)

- Spotted: The body is a color other than white, with spotting on the head and neck and white paws, tail tip, and some or all of the belly. There are three spotting patterns:

  - Classic spotting: a small spot on the nose, top of head, and nape of neck

  - Pied: a full white collar around the neck and either a spot on the nose and head or a blaze

- Mottled: Spotted or pied with attractive white spotting on the back and rump
- Other: Any other recognized color (e.g., Schimmel and Honey Cream)
- Juvenile: Any gerbil between the age of six and twelve weeks (gerbils under 6 weeks and pregnant or nursing mothers cannot be shown)
- Senior: A special class for gerbils over two years old

If you have any questions about your gerbil's color or category, the show secretary will be happy to help. An incorrectly categorized gerbil is not disqualified; instead, judges check and properly position the show pens prior to judging.

Do not speak with the judges about your gerbil before or during the competition. It is important that they not know the gerbils' kennels so they can remain impartial, because winners should be picked solely on the gerbils' merits. After the competition is over, judges are available to discuss the score sheet and how your gerbil can show better next time. Sometimes, a very nice gerbil may not place because she is still maturing, is molting into a new coat, or is a bit overweight. Maybe the class was especially competitive and while your gerbil was a high-scoring one, she placed only fourth. All of these issues can be remedied for the next show. It is important to be a good sport, whatever the outcome, and learn from the judges and from the experience.

In each category, there are two first-place (blue ribbon) winners: the highest scoring gerbil and the best gerbil of the opposite sex. First-place winners are given three points. Two points are awarded for second place and one point for third. All first-place gerbils move on to the Best in Show competition, where the judges confer to select the Best in Show and the Best of Opposite Sex winners; each are awarded an additional three points and a large, fancy ribbon called a rosette.

There are two types of "Champion" in the world of gerbil shows. An individual gerbil can become a champion by accumulating eight points in shows under at least two different judges. A gerbil kennel can earn Championship status for a color by accumulating fifteen points from wins by any gerbils of that color.

While you are at the show, be sure to meet and chat with other gerbil enthusiasts. You can see new gerbil varieties (and perhaps related species of jirds), view exhibits, and browse vendor tables for unique gerbil equipment and craft items. Some of my favorite purchases have been a magnet of "gerbil wisdoms" (such as, "Be brave, play, and take naps."), stained-glass gerbils, life-size realistic-looking gerbil ceramics, and a wooden gerbil condo with a ledge and a loft.

## Enjoy Them

Whether you have a kennel full of champion gerbils or a pair of garden-variety Agoutis, have fun with them. Pack them up and travel 500 miles to experience another part of the country and a gerbil show. Why not? Or, just stay home and watch your gerbils instead of the TV. Build a Web site featuring them. Let them inspire you to create a gerbil photograph, drawing, poem, or cartoon. Sit on the floor with them. Put together a gerbil playground or teach them to scramble up your arm and onto your shoulder. Explore the possibilities, and most of all, enjoy having your gerbils!

Gerbils are social animals that need a gerbil friend. Gerbils enjoy spending time with the special people in their lives. Some, like these two, enjoy being perched on a shoulder.

## Online Gerbil Shows

**A**N EASY WAY TO LEARN THE GERBIL SHOW STANDARDS, prepare for a live show, and experience the fun of competing is to enter your gerbil in a virtual, online fun match. All you have to do is submit clear front and side digital images of your gerbil. Points and ribbons are not awarded as in a sanctioned match, but everyone receives a write-up on the merits of the gerbil and winners are awarded a downloadable virtual ribbon, as well as glory, bragging rights, and the thrill of victory.

# Appendix

## GERBIL AND OTHER ANIMAL ORGANIZATIONS
American Gerbil Society http://www.agsgerbils.org
National Gerbil Society http://www.gerbils.co.uk/index.html
Humane Society of the United States http://www.hsus.org

## ONLINE RESOURCES FOR GERBIL CARE
http://www.agsgerbils.org/Gerbil_Care_Handbook/index.html
American Gerbil Society Gerbil Care Handbook online.
http://members.nanc.com/~mhaines/gerbil.html

### Colors and Genetics
http://home.wtal.de/ehr/gerbils/colors.htm
http://www.gerbilsuk.pwp.blueyonder.co.uk
http://www.gerbils.co.uk/gerbils/genetics.htm by Julian Barker
http://www.agsgerbils.org/Color_Strip/index.html

### Show Standards
http://www.agsgerbils.org/standards_toc.html American Gerbil
Society Judges Handbook
http://www.gerbils.pwp.blueyonder.co.uk/gerbils/standard.htm
National Gerbil Society

### Gerbil Behavior
http://home.wtal.de/ehr/gerbils/behavior.htm
http://www.awionline.org/pubs/cq02/Cq-gerb.html by Eva Waiblinger
http://www.gerbils.co.uk/gerbils/burrow.htm Compulsive Digging
by Vera Petrij Bruckmann

Gerbil Ailments

http://www.gerbils.pwp.blueyonder.co.uk/gerbils/ailments.htm

Ailments, by Jackie Roswell.

http://www.afip.org/vetpath/POLA/99/1999-POLA-Meriones.htm

Diseases of gerbils described in scientific terminology.

http://www.aspca.org/site/PageServer?pagename=apcc

ASPCA Animal Control Poison Center.

Phone: (888) 426-4435. Note: there is a fee for this service.

## RESOURCES FOR LOCATING BREEDERS AND GERBILS

http://www.agsgerbils.org/Breeders.html

http://www.petfinder.org/

http://www.agsgerbils.org/classifieds/

http://www.gerbils.co.uk/gerbils/advert.htm

## ONLINE STORES FOR GERBIL SUPPLIES AND FOOD

http://www.thatpetplace.com/

Go to the small animal, reptile, and bird pages.

http://www.petfooddirect.com/store/ Ask to get coupon e-mailings.

# BOOKS

Kotter, Engeburt. *Gerbils*. New York: Barron's Educational Series, 1999.

Discussion of gerbil behavior, care, and housing beautifully illustrated with sketches and photos.

Fox, Sue, *The guide to owning a gerbil*, Neptune City, N.J.: TFH Publications, 1993.

Accurate information about the basics of gerbil care.

Field, Karl, and Amber Sibold. *The Laboratory Hamster and Gerbil*. Boca Raton, Fla., 1999.
Contains researched-based information on gerbil physiology, nutritional needs, and husbandry requirements.

Silverstein, Alvin, and Virginia Silverstein. *Gerbils All About Them*. New York: J. B. Lippincott, 1976.
Written at the junior high level, this book provides information about gerbils from the viewpoints of a scientist and an experienced gerbil breeder. Gives details on the introduction of gerbils as pets and gerbil behavior studies that can be tried at home. Caution: never deprive a gerbil of water!

Viner, Bradley, *All About Your Gerbil*. New York: Barron's Education Series, 1999
A short, nicely illustrated book for children to learn a little bit about gerbils.

## OTHER PRINTED SOURCES

Order these printed and bound copies from http://agsgerbils.org/store.html:
*American Gerbil Society Gerbil Care Manual* (information on all aspects of gerbil care).
*American Gerbil Society Judges Manual* (includes AGS show standards with pictures of all recognized gerbil colors).
*Phoebe Sculpture* (a beautiful account of a gerbil who sculpts).

# Glossary

Agouti: brown-and-gold fur with black tips, and gray or white belly

bedding: soft substance used to make a nest and sleep in, such as unscented toilet tissue

chinchilla dust: soft powder marketed for chinchillas to take a dry dust bath

colony (or clan): all gerbils, whether related or not, living together in a housing setup

colorpoint: fur on the nose, tail, and paws darker than on the body (e.g., Siamese)

coprophagy: practice of eating feces for the vitamin B content

crepuscular: active during both day and night, with periods of activity punctuated by short naps

defense mechanisms: instinctive behaviors to ensure safety in the wild, such living in a large group, thumping a warning, digging and hiding in burrows, biting and clawing

degloving: when skin and fur on a gerbil's tail pulled off, leaving muscle and bone exposed

dominant gerbil: leader of the colony

dust bath: fluffing and rolling in chinchilla dust

food store: against the glass of a gerbil tank, gathered seed and grain—the gerbil's pantry

foraging: digging and hunting for food hidden in bedding and then carrying and burying the food in one spot in the tank (the food store)

gerbil proofing: removing hazards—such as chemicals, gerbil-size escape holes, and other pets—from a gerbil's play area outside the tank to avoid accidents

Ivermec: over-the-counter medicine used to treat mites (note: a veterinarian may be needed to dilute it to correct gerbil-size dosage)

kennel: all of an owner's gerbil colonies, even if only one

litter: 1) wood bits, corncob, or processed paper at the bottom of the cage to absorb urine and keep tank sanitary; 2) gerbil siblings born at the same time.

mites: blood-sucking gerbil parasites

molt: old hairs continually being replaced by new (some baby coats molt into different adult colors)

mottled: spotted or pied markings with additional white spotting on the back and rump

mouthing: baby gerbils exploring and learning by tasting and feeling things with their mouths (it won't hurt you—but it tickles)

nest box: a small hiding and sleeping enclosure located in one corner of the tank

nocturnal: active mostly at night (most rodents but not gerbils)

Ornacycline antibiotic: found in bird section of a pet store or online (gerbil dosage same as for small bird)

pied: full white collar and a spot on the nose and head or a blaze

quarantine: 1) period during which no animals may visit or be added to a kennel (such as several weeks prior to a show; 2) period during which new gerbils to be introduced into a kennel are kept separate from others so they may be observed to make sure they are healthy and mite free

run-around ball: hollow plastic ball about 10 inches in diameter in which the gerbil runs, protected from outside dangers

sanctioned show: an official gerbil show, judged by certified American Gerbil Society judges, in which gerbils compete for championship points

scent gland: a gland on belly used to excrete minuscule amounts of an oily substance, odorless to people but signaling "no trespassing" to other gerbils

scent marking: rubbing bellies on territory, objects, and people, especially by males, telling other gerbils, "Mine" and "Back off."

seizures (or fits): twitching and then freezing for several seconds or minutes—a natural occurrence, especially among gerbils in wild, with no long-term effects

self: belly matches the body color (e.g., black) or is one shade lighter than the body (e.g., nutmeg)

socializing: getting gerbils used to people—handled gently and frequently from a young age

split cage: used to introduce two unfamiliar gerbils or two gerbils who are separated for more than a day or two so they can smell, but not hurt or bite, each other

Tyzzers: highly contagious and fatal gerbil disease without a known cure

urinary opening: a 1/8-inch button—on the females right above the anus (bum); on the male as much as 1/2-inch between the two openings

virtual show: online show for fun only, not championship points, in which people enter their gerbils online by posting pictures. Judges may be certified or in training.

wire cloth: roll of 1/4-inch mesh wire easily cut with wire clippers and used to make a split cage

# Index

## A

activities. *See* training and activities
adults, 39, 47
aggression, 44, 47
aging, 106–107
American Gerbil Society, 20, 78, 105, 131, 148, 152, 156; list of breeders, 34; memorials, 107; online classifieds, 38; placement recommendations, 129

## B

Barker, Julian, 82
bathing, 61, 92, 158
bedding (litter), 58, 94–95, 117
behaviors: aggressive, 26; biting/nipping, 80, 86–88; copying, 140; defensive/protective, 12; dominant/submissive, 44, 47, 52–53; foot thumping, 12, 78; grooming, 53; mating, 15; purring, 82; scent-marking, 11; territorial, 24–25, 82; typical, 58; undesirable, 87, 141; in the wild, 13. *See also* handling
biting/nipping, 26, 80, 86–88
Blocke, Judith H., 136
breeders lists, 34
breeding: birthing, 121–122; emergency birthing kits, 117–118; fostering, 122–124; housing for, 115–117; inbreeding, 115; limited breeding, 130–131; litters, 58, 111, 122; mating, 118–120; planned, 114–115; prenatal care, 120; pup development, 124–128; questions to ask before, 111–112; separating males/females, 130; unplanned pregnancies, 112–113; weaning, 128–130
buying gerbils: accessories, 23–24; color, 40; costs, 23–24; gender/sexing, 41–44; how many to get, 44, 47; individual selection, 38–40; questions for, 20, 42; shopping list for, 58; where to find, 33–38

## C

cages. *See* housing
care and maintenance: bathing, 61, 92, 158; cleaning cages, 24, 65–68, 117, 158; hand washing, 78; irresponsible, 40; mite control, 101–102; time required, 24. *See also* feeding
catching escaped gerbils, 85–86
characteristics of gerbils, 11, 39, 154
chewing, 15, 64

children, 26–27, 88
choosing your gerbil. *See* buying gerbils
classroom suitability, 27–28
color(s): available, 43; breeding for, 114–115; choosing, 40; description of, 45; show standards, 154–155; varieties, 10; in the wild, 13–14
costs, 23–24, 36

## D

dangers (to gerbils): children, 26–27; food items, 58; handling pups, 122; household hazards, 68–69; improper location of enclosures, 22; introducing gerbils, 49–50; to newborns, 113, 129; other pets, 24–26; poisoning, 103; of separation, 158; tail injuries, 86, 97; from toys, 64. *See also* diseases/disorders
dangers (to humans): biting/nipping, 26, 80, 86–88; children handling gerbils, 26–27; fighting gerbils, 49, 53; legal issues, 31
Davies, Deborah, 28
death, 105, 107–108, 114
defecation, 98, 105–106
dehydration, 30, 71–72, 96, 120
diet. *See* feeding
diseases/disorders: administering medications, 99; aging, 106–107; allergies, 94–95; broken limbs, 96; cysts, 102–103; death, 107–108; dehydration, 96, 120; diarrhea, 98, 105–106; ear cysts and infections, 100; emergency medical kits, 94; head injuries, 96; health, signs of, 42; health checklist, 93; heat stroke, 98–99; hypothermia, 99–100; from inbreeding, 115; kinked tails/wrists, 100–101; parasites, 40, 101–102; prevention, 92; respiratory infections, 104, 117; seizures, 12, 16, 104; signs of good/ill health, 92–93; strokes, 105; tail injuries, 97; teeth, 96; tumors, 103; tyzzers, 105–106; vitamin B deficiency, 65; during weaning, 131; weight gain/obesity, 71. *See also* dangers (to gerbils)

## E

ears/hearing, 78, 100
educational exhibits, 147–148, 149–152
emergencies, 94, 105, 117–118. *See also* diseases/disorders
entertainment, 133–135